THE
NATURAL

Also by Joe Klein

Fiction
Primary Colors
The Running Mate

Nonfiction
Woody Guthrie: A Life
Payback: Five Marines After Vietnam

THE
NATURAL

The Misunderstood Presidency
of
BILL
CLINTON

JOE KLEIN

BROADWAY BOOKS New York

The Library of Congress has cataloged the Doubleday
hardcover edition as follows:
Klein, Joe, 1946–
The natural / Joe Klein.—1st ed.
p.   cm.
Includes index.
1. Clinton, Bill, 1946–   2. Clinton, Bill, 1946—Ethics.
3. Presidents—United States—Biography.   4. United States—
Politics and government—1993–2001.   5. Political corruption—
United States—History—20th century.   I. Title.

E886 .K64 2002
973.929'092—dc21
[B]
2001047428

ISBN 0-7679-1412-0

5 7 9 10 8 6 4

In the spring of 1992, in the midst of the New York primary, I dragged my five-year-old daughter, Sophie, to see Bill Clinton speak at a town meeting at Co-op City in the Bronx. It was a raucous affair, a barrage of angry, detailed questions from retired trade unionists and other assorted skeptics. Clinton was in the midst of a rough patch, under assault from the New York tabloids and also from the liberal intelligentsia—Jerry Brown, the former governor of California, was the chic protest vote of the moment. I had piled on, too, with a column in *New York* magazine about the fudges and inconsistencies in his campaign. But when Clinton saw Sophie standing with me as he made his way out of the hall, he came over, squatted down, put a big hand on my daughter's shoulder, and said, "Sophie, I know that your father hasn't been home much these past few months. He's been with me . . . but he talks about you *all the time*."

This book is dedicated to Sophie and Teddy Klein, as an explanation of, and an apology for, the months and years I wasn't there.

He was so extremely natural that there was no knowing what his
nature was, or what came next.
—*George Santayana on William James*

Prologue

On January 21, 1998, after five tumultuous, sloppy, often brilliant, exhausting—and elusive—years as President of the United States, Bill Clinton finally landed in a political mess from which he seemed unlikely to extricate himself. That morning, the *Washington Post* reported the President apparently had been intimate with a White House intern, a young woman named Monica Lewinsky—and that he had lied about this relationship under oath (in a sexual harassment lawsuit brought by a second woman, a former Arkansas state employee named Paula Corbin Jones). The news was received with undisguised glee by the national press, which had repeatedly chased the President down dark alleys of imagined corruption only to find the trails evaporate and the alleged perpetrator basking in what seemed to be illogical levels of public approval. *These* charges, however, were considerably more accessible (and more plausible) than the previous run of misdemeanors. They combined the President's most commonly assumed depravities: a surplus of libido and a deficit of integrity. The surplus had been expended upon an employee the approximate age of his daughter, and the deficit involved untruthfulness of a potentially criminal sort. Furthermore, there appeared to be solid evidence of Clinton's guilt. There were tape recordings—the second time in his career that Clinton had allowed himself to be caught on tape in intimate conversations with a woman not his wife. And there were rumors of more revelations to come. That morning, George Stephanopoulos—formerly Clinton's closest personal aide but now a professional commentator on the ABC television network—had opened the bidding at the highest possible level: He speculated that these charges were so serious that, if proven, they would lead to impeachment proceedings.

The first televised images of the President that day were startling. For once, this most facile of politicians seemed flummoxed: He looked tired, blotchy, shifty, nervously parsing tenses—"There *is* no relationship"—in an interview with Jim Lehrer of public television on the afternoon the story appeared. Then, a few days later, as rumors spread that he was about to resign, Clinton betrayed a rare flash of public anger. He shook his finger at the cameras and uttered the words that would define his presidency for many: "I did not have sexual relations with that woman—Miss Lewinsky."

If the President seemed a bit unhinged in public, a more subtle drama was being enacted behind the scenes: Clinton may have been reeling, but he was also beginning to organize a survival strategy. His first task was to convince his staff that the presidency wasn't crumbling. The appearance of business as usual was crucial. Consequently, only a handful of lawyers and political advisors were detached to deal with the scandal, and they were isolated from the rest of the President's team; most everyone else, including Clinton himself, continued working— with a stubborn, purposeful myopia—on the substance of the office, which, that week, was the preparation of the annual State of the Union message.

Clinton never mentioned Monica Lewinsky as he proceeded with this work, but his associates found it difficult, at times, to focus on the task at hand. Televisions are ubiquitous in the

White House, usually tuned to the all-news networks; now they were broadcasting nonstop mayhem—the chaos was just a few doors away in the press room, a near riot at the briefing held each afternoon by the press secretary, Mike McCurry, as well as constant, breathless bulletins from the row of television reporters stationed just outside, on the North Lawn. The proximity of the disaster was difficult to assimilate; the West Wing—usually a pretty quiet place, given the seriousness of the work and the thickness of the carpets—was even more hushed than usual. Looks and shrugs were exchanged in the cramped hallways, but not many words. It was obvious to all but the most credulous that Clinton was probably lying, but what was there to say?

The President's relationship with his staff was as complicated as the rest of his life. Awe and disappointment were intertwined. The awe was inspired by Clinton's intelligence—particularly, his encyclopedic knowledge of policy questions—his perseverance and his ability to charm almost anyone under any circumstances; he was, without question, the most talented politician of his generation. At close range, his skills could be breathtaking: He was always the center of attention; he filled any room he entered. But there was a harshness, a certain brute insensitivity that was inextricably part of these fluorescent energies. All of Clinton's emotional sensitivity seemed to be expended in his work, which meant that there was not much decency or graciousness left over for the help. His self-involvement, self-indulgence, and, all too often, self-pity, were notorious. And yet, the staff was intensely loyal, with a deep sense of political mission. There had not been a truly successful Democratic administration in a very long time; Clinton was the first Democrat to win reelection to a second term since Franklin Roosevelt. The ideological extremism of the Republican opposition and the media's persistent, often niggling, campaign to prove the President corrupt only confirmed the high stakes: The Administration seemed perpetually embattled and the White House staff had been trained to react swiftly, with lethal force, to attacks on the President. This avidity was not to be confused with personal affection for the man.

In the days after the Lewinsky scandal began, however, the staff was the object—for once—of a virtuoso Clinton performance. He needed his people to be loyal, to continue to work hard, to not be discouraged. He would lead by example; he would astonish them with his ability to keep his focus, despite the overwhelming distractions. One day, for example, Michael Waldman, the chief speechwriter, was paged by the President as he sat in his office watching television: McCurry was being pummeled with questions about new rumors of an imminent resignation. Waldman wondered if he was about to be asked to write the final Clinton speech. But the President didn't even seem to be *aware* of the mayhem in the press room. He was calling about the State of the Union message, specifically about a memo he had received from Stephen Carter, the Yale University law professor. "Did you check out Carter's language for the 'Idea of America' section?" Clinton asked casually. "Try to work it in."

In his most private moments, of course, the President wasn't quite so stalwart. Gradually, the news spread of anguished one-on-one conversations with his closest advisors, including his wife—outrageous conversations, in which Clinton denied his involvement with the young woman and even suggested that Lewinsky had been "stalking" him. There was an odd, dispirited Super Bowl party that weekend, attended by the Reverend Jesse Jackson—a frequent and sometimes bitter Clinton rival in the past, now a sudden confidant; Jackson stayed on afterward to pray with the President, and to console his wife and daughter. Clinton's old friend, the television producer Harry Thomasson, flew in from California to help with the crisis. Almost all the details that proved, astonishingly, true—the semen-stained dress, the banal gifts (dreadful gifts, the sort of things one adolescent would give to another: T-shirts, assorted ticky-tack, and a copy of Walt Whitman's *Leaves of Grass*), the passionate late-night phone calls, the inference that oral sex might not count as sex— all became known during those first few days.

But the President also spent hours rehearsing, rewriting, and sometimes rethinking sections of the State of the Union. At these times, Clinton appeared able to lose himself in the work; after a shaky first day or two, he didn't even seem particularly depressed or distracted. "The thing I remember is how smoothly everything seemed to go, more so than in other years," said Sylvia Mathews, the deputy chief of staff whose job it was to keep the speech on track. "We were rehearsing in the Family Theater the weekend before the speech was to be delivered. Usually, he didn't get to full-scale dress rehearsal until the day of the speech. But he was up there, working real hard, extremely focused, rewriting the sections on education and race. He showed up on Saturday with a draft covered with his left-handed scrawls: It was obvious he'd spent the night before working on the text.

He'd say things like, 'I've cut out fifteen words here and added a paragraph. Listen to this . . .' Everything had to get better and better, tighter and tighter."

Over time, Clinton had transformed the State of the Union ritual into more than just a speech. It was now a six-month policy-making process, a central organizing tool for his substantive agenda in any given year. The President believed the speech was his best chance to communicate in an unfiltered way with the American people (usually at mind-numbing length: He'd routinely prattle on well past the hour traditionally set aside by the television networks). The media, inevitably, would deride these gargantuan efforts, but the public seemed to love them, which made the annual exercise all the more satisfying for the President. And so, great care was taken: Briefing books were prepared; wish lists compiled by each department; policy options considered. There was a discipline to the process that must have seemed odd to old friends of the scattered, garrulous Bill Clinton. But this was a different White House from the floating bull session of the first term; and this was a different Clinton—more reserved, more dignified, more consciously presidential (most of the time). Indeed, as he stood behind the "Blue Goose"—his full-dress lectern—in the Family Theater that Saturday and rehearsed his lines before much of his staff, Bill Clinton may have been the only person in the room wearing a jacket and tie.

THE PRESIDENT AND HIS ECONOMIC team had spent most of their energy that year trying to think through a novel political conundrum. In 1997, Clinton had negotiated a balanced budget with the Republican majority in Congress and now, for the first time in forty years, there was the prospect of a surplus. The Republicans wanted that money for a tax cut. "But everyone knew that the budget wasn't really balanced," Robert Rubin, who was then Treasury Secretary, would recall. "Surpluses were being projected—not the sort of surpluses we eventually got; no one saw those coming at that point—but we also expected that discretionary spending was likely to exceed the forecast. A tax cut would probably throw us back into deficits. We had a series of meetings, starting in October, searching for a strategy. I think it was John Hilley"—a presidential aide in charge of legislative affairs—"who first came up with the idea of using the surplus to preserve Social Security."

Hilley's idea was passed along to Mark Penn, the President's pollster. This was standard operating procedure in the Clinton White House, which spent more money on polling than all previous administrations combined. Not only was every significant policy idea tested, the language that would be used to introduce each new idea was tested, too. Happily, in this case, Penn reported that the public seemed far more interested in preserving its old-age pensions than it was in receiving a tax cut—and this would be the grand oratorical ploy of the 1998 State of the Union message. The President would oppose a tax cut in an election year.

Clinton wanted to take this stand in the most dramatic way possible; his speechwriters were having difficulty coming up with the right words, though. Then, in the midst of the Saturday rehearsal, as he reached the point where he asked the rhetorical question "What should we do with our new surplus?" Clinton suddenly interrupted himself and said, "Hey, I've got an idea! How about this: 'I have a simple four-word answer. Save Social Security First.' "

The President stopped and smiled. The staff applauded. Then he waved his arms out broadly, and said, "See, I haven't *totally* lost it."

INDEED, MANY OF THOSE CLOSEST to Bill Clinton believed that he had only recently found "it"—that he had just begun to master the presidency. This was one of the more distressing aspects of the Lewinsky scandal: He had finally regained his political confidence after a chaotic, often inept, first term filled with abstract victories and concrete defeats—Mrs. Clinton's failed and foolish attempt at health insurance reform was, for example, far more palpable than her husband's revolutionary effort to eradicate the federal budget deficit. He had learned how to get what he wanted from a Republican Congress in the complicated, end-of-session budget negotiations; he had successfully used military force in Bosnia and was now more comfortable as commander in chief; he had taken the measure of other world leaders and was increasingly confident on the international stage. "He had stopped acting like a governor," said Donna Shalala, the Secretary of Health and Human Services, "and he had become the President."

But he was a confounding President. His presidency seemed to proceed simultaneously on two competing, dissonant tracks—policy and personality—the latter usually overwhelming the former, particularly in Washington. The general public tended to react more positively toward Clinton than did the political community: favoring his policies, impressed by his gifts, bemused by his personal indulgences. But Clinton had few true allies in Washington; not many politicians, not even in his own party, felt entirely comfortable with him. And he had a terrible relationship with the press. He had come to power at a particularly brutal moment in the history of American public life; his ascension marked the climax of a twenty-year period of lethal partisan warfare, which had begun with Richard Nixon's forced resignation from the presidency and had been punctuated by an ever-escalating series of political show trials and soap operas involving alleged (often trivial) misbehavior by public officials. His ascension also marked the arrival of a new generation to political power: the Baby Boomers, born after World War II. Indeed, Bill Clinton often seemed the apotheosis of his generation's alleged sins: the moral relativism, the tendency to pay more attention to marketing than to substance, the solipsistic callowness.

Many of Clinton's Republican opponents would never accept his legitimacy as President. He had decisively defeated George Bush in 1992 and Bob Dole in 1996, but he had received less than a pure majority of the vote in both elections because of the presence of a third candidate, the Independent Ross Perot (the Republicans seem even more intemperate in retrospect, given their vehement and immediate assertions of George W. Bush's victory in the dead-heat campaign of 2000). The press, always more interested in scandal than in substance, seemed to have a particularly difficult time establishing the proper proportion between the two during the Clinton years: Even the most responsible newspapers and networks appeared obsessed with the

President's personal failings. Minuscule imbroglios—like the attempt to fire several career employees in the White House Travel Office—and standard political maneuverings (the tendency to do business with, and grant favors to, campaign contributors when he was governor of Arkansas) were blown up into major political crises, which were exacerbated by Clinton's attempts to lawyer, and occasionally lie, his way out of trouble. It was said that he had no core principles, that he was too "slick" to be trusted—and there was some truth to that.

In fact, Bill Clinton was strangely malleable, a creature of his audience, besotted with his ability to charm, constantly trying to please. This worked to his advantage during election campaigns and State of the Union messages, when the audience was the American people. But it could be a disastrous quality when the audience was smaller—when he fixed upon the priorities and prejudices of the sclerotic Democrats who ran the Congress early in his administration; or when he (rather understandably) allowed himself to be distracted by the obsessions of the media or the special prosecutors investigating him. It was even worse when he inhabited the needs of the sycophants and fund-raisers and favor-seekers who inevitably clot around power—when he indulged their vanity with access, with personal photos and coffees and overnight stays in the Lincoln Bedroom. And worst of all was when he allowed himself to believe their flattery and succumbed to their importunings—at the very end of his time in office, when he allowed these "friends" to convince him to issue presidential pardons to their less-than-savory acquaintances. Clinton's two most important audiences—the American people and the writers of history—were, obviously, nowhere on the radar screen his last night in office, when he decided to pardon 177 individuals, including a disgraced financier named Marc Rich, who had fled the country and was prominent on the Federal Bureau of Investigation's Ten Most Wanted list.

In the end, the only three Clinton quotations judged memorable enough to be included in the seventeenth edition of *Bartlett's Familiar Quotations,* published a year after he left office, were:

"I experimented with marijuana a time or two. And I didn't like it, and didn't inhale, and didn't try it again."—3/31/92

"I am going to say this again: I did not have sexual relations with that woman—Miss Lewinsky."—1/26/98

"It depends on what the meaning of the word 'is' is. If the—if he—if 'is' means is and never has been, that is not—that is one thing. If it means there is none, that was a completely true statement."—8/17/98

AND YET, IT COULD *ALSO* be argued—despite Clinton's gaudy personal failings—that he had run a serious, disciplined, responsible presidency. "If you see a turtle sitting on top of a fence post," Clinton would often say, "it didn't get there by accident." A quotation worthy of *Bartlett's,* by which he meant that the historic prosperity and the global peace that attended his time in office were not accidental. They were, at least in part, attributable to thousands of decisions—subtle, nuanced, complicated, often risky decisions—that Clinton and his advisors had made over the years, decisions that lacked the neon explosiveness of the Lewinsky scandal or the Marc Rich pardon, but which were the true work of the presidency.

Furthermore, it can be argued that the reason Bill Clinton succeeded as well as he did in the substance of his presidency is that—intellectually, at least—he was quite the opposite of the slickster his enemies imagined: He arrived in Washington with a coherent, sophisticated political vision, which he pursued rigorously, quite often in ways that were politically inexpedient in the short term. He had, by turns, alienated traditional liberals, conservatives, and moderates, but his heresies were schematic. The apparent contradictions in Clinton's agenda—support for free trade (which should have pleased conservatives) and for universal health insurance (which should have pleased liberals); support for welfare reform (which appalled liberals) and for affirmative action (which appalled conservatives)—were all part of what he considered to be his larger mission: to manage the nation's transition from the Industrial Age to the Information Age.

He had been proposing that as his political project for years—he'd first broached it with me in the late 1980s, when he was still governor of Arkansas, well before he decided when he would actually run for President—but to most ears, the formulation "from the Industrial Age to the Information Age" seemed grandiose at best; it sounded like political boilerplate culled from focus groups. . . . or worse, messianic Baby Boom hooey. (It was no accident that the other American politician retailing the notion of a "historic" economic paradigm shift back in the

1980s, and who used almost the exact same words as Clinton did, was Newt Gingrich.)

Clinton's ultimate success in this project was mixed, at best. But he never received credit for the essential coherence of his vision because he never found a way to articulate it credibly, much less succinctly—no small irony, given his ability to communicate. He wasn't even sure what to call the program. He had tried "The New Choice" in 1991 and then "The New Covenant" during the 1992 campaign. He called himself a "New Democrat." He spoke incessantly, and appallingly, about "building a bridge to the twenty-first century" during his 1996 campaign (at his second inauguration, a model of that bridge had been built on the Mall, paved with AstroTurf). His final attempt, destined to be only marginally more successful than the others—except overseas, where it became the rallying cry of former leftists who had discovered the inevitability of the global marketplace—was to call his philosophy "The Third Way."

As Clinton prepared his 1998 State of the Union message, the economic transformation he had long predicted—from the Industrial Age to the Information Age—was finally beginning to seem something more than a rhetorical conceit. The national economy was behaving in ways that had seemed unimaginable a few years earlier. Unemployment rates were plummeting while inflation rates remained at historic lows; prosperity was rising at all income levels (the incomes of households in the broad middle of the economic spectrum increased by a remarkable 35 percent during his eight years in office). Traditional notions of time and space and borders were being challenged by new technologies—portable computers, the Internet, cell phones, satellite television—that were simultaneously transforming not only the global marketplace, but also the most routine ceremonies of middle-class life.

This was a transformation, Clinton believed, similar to the development, at the beginning of the twentieth century, of a truly national economy dominated by vast corporate trusts. At that time, the federal government—led by Theodore Roosevelt and Woodrow Wilson, the two presidents Clinton had hoped to emulate—responded to the economic change by enacting a series of historic reforms to harness the new economy (everything from the passage of a Pure Food and Drug Act to the imposition of an income tax and the creation of the Federal Reserve System). Clinton believed his task was to enact a similar series of reforms, appropriate to the Information Age. But, as he prepared for the 1998 State of the Union message, the President could point to no single accomplishment as grand as those of Roosevelt and Wilson. By force of personality and sheer persistence, he had slowly dragged Washington toward a recognition that a revised form of government activism might be appropriate in the anarchy of an instant economy—but he had won his victories in dribs and drabs; his defeats had been far more memorable.

Clinton was, of course, a fabulous talker. In some ways, he was a better public speaker—because of his intellectual acuity, his informality, his ability to improvise—than Ronald Reagan had been; he was the President most comfortable behind a podium since John Kennedy. (Newt Gingrich, Clinton's most vehement Republican opponent, once told me he'd sat through a Clinton State of the Union speech thinking, "We're dead. There's no way we're going to beat this guy.") But the President's oratorical strength was mostly a consequence of his physical presence, a mirage of body language. He seemed incapable of memorable rhetoric; he had never found a way to communicate his larger purpose to the American public, and this was a source of enduring frustration to him.

At first, the 1998 State of the Union message appeared to be the perfect moment to take another crack at it—and there were several paragraphs, near the beginning of the address, that were as lucid a statement of his political philosophy as he'd ever attempted. But, after the Lewinsky scandal began, the sole purpose of the speech became to insure his political survival (even the Social Security bombshell was destined to be lost in the melodrama). He had decided not to mention the scandal at all that night; indeed, the fabulously self-destructive "I did not sleep with that woman" statement on the day before the speech had been a planned preemptive strike—suggested by his friend Harry Thomasson—a foolish attempt to clear the air before his State of the Union address. The air would not be cleared, however. The Lewinsky subtext was everywhere; his staff spent hours scouring the final text for potentially embarrassing *double entendres*.

THERE WAS APPLAUSE AS THE President made his way into the chamber of the House of Representatives just after nine o'clock on the evening of January 27, 1998. He was greeted warmly, defiantly, by the Democrats who gathered near the center aisle to shake his hand. This had become one of the odder features of the Clinton dynamic: The left wing of the

Democratic Party, which had suffered through his assorted ideological heresies, was never so supportive of the President as when he was involved in a scandal. "What kept us close to the President was the Republicans," said Senator Charles Schumer of New York, who was still a member of the House in 1998. "Their extreme nastiness pushed Democrats into Bill Clinton's arms, even those who didn't like him very much."

There were very few House Democrats who could be said to like Clinton at all. Most members of Congress represented narrow, homogenous constituencies; the Democrats tended toward anachronistic Industrial Age liberalism. Just a few weeks earlier, the House leadership had seemed on the brink of outright rebellion against the President—Minority Leader Richard Gephardt had complained, in a speech at Harvard, about Clinton's willingness to compromise with the conservatives in the budget negotiations of 1997, on welfare reform and free trade. In October, the Democrats had voted overwhelmingly against giving the President "fast track" authority to negotiate new trade agreements. "He was tremendously upset by that," said a foreign policy advisor. "He considered the vote a massive and very personal 'Fuck you, Bill Clinton.' "

But now, Monica Lewinsky—of all people—had forced the Democrats back into the fold. They stood and cheered as the President reached the podium. And they cheered again as he opened his speech with an impressive barrage of statistics: "We have fourteen million new jobs; the lowest unemployment in twenty-four years; the lowest core inflation in thirty years; incomes are rising and we have the highest home ownership in history. Crime has dropped for a record five years in a row. And the welfare rolls are at their lowest levels in twenty-seven years. Our leadership in the world is unrivaled. Ladies and gentlemen"—he paused, slowing down for the ritual pronouncement—"the state of our union is strong."

He lowered his voice on "strong," delivering it like a hammer blow rather than a trumpet clarion. After savoring the applause—even the Republicans had to join in—he moved on to his statement of creed: "Rarely have Americans lived through so much change, in so many ways, in so short a time. . . . We have moved into an Information Age, a global economy, a truly new world.

"For five years now we have met the challenge of these changes at every turning point. . . . We have moved past the sterile debate of those who say government is the enemy and those who say government is the answer. My fellow Americans, we have found a Third Way. We have the smallest government in thirty-five years, but a more progressive one. We have a smaller government, but a stronger nation." He was interrupted here by ironic applause from the Republicans. But he pressed on, reciting the three principles of The Third Way: opportunity, responsibility and community—words that Clinton had made the slogan of the moderate Democratic Leadership Council when he became its chairman in 1991. Ever since, politicians from Tony Blair in England to George W. Bush in Texas had used the same words to win elections; by 1998, however, the formulation was beginning to seem hackneyed and, in revisiting it, the President lost steam. He made a last attempt to summarize his governing philosophy, offering a three-point "strategy for prosperity: fiscal discipline to cut interest rates and spur growth; investments in education and skills . . . to prepare our people for the new economy; new markets for American products and American workers."

This was the heart of his governing philosophy, succinctly put, but there was no applause. The words were too abstract; there was nothing stirring or striking or controversial about them. The Third Way—which, in practice, challenged both liberal and conservative orthodoxies—could sound like Everyone's Way when massaged into platitudes by a decent speechwriter. Clinton's next statement, however, brought an explosion of bipartisan cheers: "For three decades, six presidents have come before you to warn of the damage deficits pose to our nation. Tonight, I come before you to announce that the federal deficit—once so incomprehensibly large that it had eleven zeros—will be, simply, zero."

The President basked in the cheers, his jaw set, smiling slightly. For a moment, the Lewinsky business seemed very far away. And now, he was ready to take his big gamble: "If we balance the budget for next year, it is projected that we'll have a sizable surplus in the years that immediately follow. What should we do with this projected surplus?" He paused for effect. "I have a simple four word answer: Save . . . Social . . . Security . . . First!"

The Democrats were up, out of their seats with a roar. Newt Gingrich, the Republican Speaker of the House, who sat directly above and behind the President, was applauding, too, but reluctantly, and he was still seated. Slowly, Gingrich seemed to understand that he had been snookered yet again by Bill Clinton—that the nation would see Democrats vigorously supporting the most popular federal program, Social Security, while the Republicans were still seated, glumly—and he hauled himself to his feet and joined in a standing ovation for the President of the United States.

"It was, to my mind, the most incredible moment of the presidency," the speechwriter, Michael Waldman, would remember. "Not so much because Clinton had managed to outthink and outflank the Republicans in the midst of the Lewinsky scandal, but because in that moment you could just see one trillion dollars moving from their side of the ledger to ours, from tax cuts to Social Security."

NOT MANY PEOPLE NOTICED, THOUGH.

"The big news that night was that I was standing there," Bill Clinton would recall years later, in one of a series of conversations he and I had at the end of his eight years in office. He was eager to make a case for the successes of his administration; but he was also quite candid, at times, about his substantive failures. He was wistful about opportunities lost, and infuriated—at himself, but mostly at his enemies—over the time wasted in scandals. The meaning of his administration had been obscured. "I'm not sure," he said, "that I ever took full advantage of the opportunity to lay the coherent philosophy out."

Our first conversation was oddly formal. We sat at a glass coffee table in a small room that seemed an afterthought in a styleless New York hotel suite (the President was in town for a speech). Clinton was wearing a dark blue suit, red tie, and white shirt, a generic outfit. His demeanor was similarly reserved. He remained seated for more than two hours, never took off his jacket and never raised his voice, even when he was excited or angered by a question. After an hour of talking, he asked a steward for a decaffeinated coffee and a glass of water. He didn't offer me—or any of his staff aides present—anything to drink; indeed, he didn't make much of an effort at all to charm me. He rarely laughed or even smiled, although he did loosen up a bit when I asked if there was a moment in 1998, the Lewinsky year, when it suddenly became to clear to him that all of his first-term policy gambles—higher taxes, budget discipline, welfare reform, freer trade—were paying off. "Was there a bolt of lightning?" I asked.

"Well, there were plenty of lightning bolts that year," Clinton said with a laugh, stretching out his long legs. "But they were all aimed at me. I spent a lot of ninety-eight wrestling with three overwhelming feelings. There was obviously a lot of pain involved, because I had made a terrible personal mistake, which I didn't try to correct until almost a year later—and I had to live with it, and it caused an enormous amount of pain to my family, to my administration, to the country. And then I had to deal with what the Republicans wanted to do with it. . . . I really believed I was defending the Constitution. . . . I still believe that two of the great achievements of my administration were facing down the government shutdowns"—which were the result of a first-term budget impasse with the Republicans—"and this." He didn't use the word impeachment; it was almost as if he wouldn't dignify the Republican campaign against him with so dignified and *constitutional* a word. "Those two things together essentially ended the most overt and extreme manifestations of the Gingrich revolution."

The President sat back, and seemed to relax a bit. "And the third thing I felt that year was, 'Gosh, it's all working! It's all coming together.' . . . I was really happy. I was happy because I thought—to be fair, I don't think any of us ever thought in ninety-three that the economy would take off this way."

That remarkable year, 1998, crystallized the Clinton conundrum: solid policy and brilliant politics obscured by the consequences of tawdry personal behavior. The vituperative pettiness of those years, the irresponsibility on all sides, seem almost foreign now after the violent events that have overwhelmed the presidency of George W. Bush. Bill Clinton was lucky to serve as President in such quiet times, times he palpably made better through his economic and domestic policy actions, but he was also unlucky: He was never challenged in a way that tested his impressive strengths, and the absence of a challenge exacerbated his distressing weaknesses. Perhaps now, in a different century and a different world, a more accurate assessment of the policy, the politics—and of the person himself—can be made.

CHAPTER
ONE

Beneath a khaki sky on a brisk, desolate weekday morning just after Christmas 1991, Bill Clinton's mother gave me a tour of Hot Springs, Arkansas, the town where she had raised her two boys through a succession of family melodramas. Virginia Kelley was an unlikely, but wonderfully American, candidate to be the mother of a President. She was the sort of woman whom proper folks tend to scorn, particularly in the South: a ton of makeup, almost comically applied; a white streak down the middle of her dyed black hair (some of the locals called her "skunk woman"); a passion for the racetrack, for nightlife—Hot Springs had been a notorious Bible Belt Gomorrah—and for the wrong sort of men. And yet, Mrs. Kelley was not at all pathetic; she was canny and formidable and charming; an entertaining guide who, in the course of our day together, managed to ask all the right political questions and also to make some very astute predictions. "I think the press is going to give Bill a lot of trouble." She sighed. "Don't you?"

At one point she startled me. "That's the church where I go to my A.A. meetings," she said, nodding toward a prim Protestant outpost of recent vintage.

"Are you—"

"An alcoholic?" she interrupted me. "No, but I had one for a husband and a drug addict for a son—and I get a certain amount of comfort from the meetings."

This was not entirely convincing. She had the leathery look of a woman who knew her way around a cocktail lounge. But the attempted subterfuge wasn't nearly as important as the door opened by her admission: Mrs. Kelley lived in the twelve-step world. She was practiced in a stylized, jargon-buffered sort of candor. She proceeded to tell me horrific stories, all of which she had undoubtedly rehearsed sitting with her fellow fallen in a circle of metal folding chairs in the linoleum-and-cinderblock church basement (most of the stories had not been divulged to the press before, though). She told me about guns brandished about the house and accidentally fired by her alcoholic husband, Roger, who was Bill's stepfather. She told me about the time Bill had smashed through the bedroom door and stopped her drunken husband from abusing her. She told me that she and Bill and her younger son, Roger, had gone into family therapy together after Roger was busted for cocaine (while Bill was governor; the surveillance and arrest took place with Bill's prior approval).

The last was an admission that I didn't appreciate sufficiently at the time: Bill Clinton was the first American President to admit that he had participated in a form of psychotherapy. One imagines him totally cooperative, wildly eloquent, emotionally accessible, flagrantly remorseful . . . and completely in control of the situation, three steps ahead of the therapist—the analysand from hell.

Several days later, as I traveled with Clinton through New Hampshire—he was in the process of taking that first primary state by storm (a process snuffed a few weeks later by the twin revelations that he'd had an extramarital affair with a lounge singer and that he'd not quite told the truth about his efforts to avoid military service in Vietnam)—I asked Clinton what he'd learned in family therapy, and whether it had been odd growing up in a family where the two career paths turned out to be getting elected governor and becoming a cocaine addict.

"Well," he said without hesitation, "there are different sorts of addictions."

By which I assumed he meant—I was, quite frankly, too embarrassed to pursue this very aggressively—that his addiction was to fame and success and glory. Of course, even if I had pursued it, Clinton undoubtedly would have used some brilliant tactic to skitter away (at least, that's how I now rationalize my journalistic incompetence). But the conversation did establish an important subtext for Clinton's success as a politician in the 1990s: his thorough mastery of the therapeutic vocabulary and the *trompe l'oeil* sense of intimacy it provided.

Certainly, I'd never met a politician like him before. I barely knew the man and we were talking, or seeming to talk, about the most ridiculously intimate things. This set a certain tone, and some rather strange parameters, for the relationship that evolved between us. I probably should say a few words about that.

We had met a few years earlier. He was immediately impressive. He seemed to know everything there was to know about domestic social policy. "Just remarkable," David Osborne, the author of *Laboratories of Democracy*, a book about some of the more successful state governors in the 1980s, once told me. "You call him up and ask, 'Who's doing interesting things in housing?' And he can tell you what *everyone* is doing—every last housing experiment in every state."

I had similar conversations with Clinton early on—about education and welfare reform and the impact of globalization on the national economy. As a result, our relationship was quite good at first. It turned chillier during the course of his campaign for the presidency in 1992, and then it became very cold indeed during his first two years as President, as he appeared to abandon the moderate path he had set for himself in the campaign; finally, toward the end of his years in office, we had a rapprochement. Our differences—or rather, my criticisms (he never complained directly to me about anything I said or wrote)—were often harsh and sometimes inappropriate, but almost always over matters of substance.

We were, in fact, from the same part of the ideological jungle: a rather obscure, eclectic tribe known as the "New Democrats"—the vagueness of that designation made my attempts to enforce a philosophical rigor on him all the more ridiculous—but neither of us was very comfortable there. The conventions of journalism prevented me from ever fitting too neatly into any political niche (although, as a columnist for *New York* magazine, *Newsweek*, and *The New Yorker*, my predilections were obvious to most readers). As for Clinton, he was too good a politician to be confined: He expanded the definition of a New Democrat to include anyone who might at some point vote for him. Over time, this infuriated almost everyone involved in the Democratic Party's perpetual internecine wars.

So I'd written favorably about him, with a few notable exceptions—most involving his shameless fudging and jiving on the campaign trail—when he'd run for President in 1992. I was more critical when he seemed to slouch leftward during the first few years of his presidency: away from welfare reform and education reform, toward a clumsy, anachronistic health insurance scheme and, not least, by surrounding himself with some very high-profile Old Democrats in both the cabinet and the West Wing—during the first few years of his presidency. And then, in 1996, my anonymous novel called *Primary Colors* was published. It caused something of a sensation and was considered, incorrectly to my mind, an attack on the President. Actually, I had come to a more benign point of view while writing the book: I saw it as a defense of larger-than-life politicians—who, inevitably, have mythic weaknesses entangled with their obvious strengths. In the end, it seemed obvious that a larger-than-life leader was preferable to one who was smaller than life. It also was becoming clear—sadly so, I thought—that "larger than life" was a difficult personality type for a politician in the Information Age: The media's perpetual, uninflected and cynical puritanism exaggerated the flaws and neutered the strengths. (*Primary Colors* was intended to be as much about the witless intensity of life in the spotlight, and the velocity of modern politics, as it was about the nature of the people who succeed in the arena.)

Happily, Clinton seemed to be able to float above the barrage—he was the world's biggest, fattest target, but somehow managed to keep himself impervious to assault. As a public performer, he was mesmerizing, maddening, transcendent. He dominated a brutal political landscape so completely as to make my ideological quibbles appear foolish; and his more serious political opponents were continually frustrated by his buoyancy and appalled by his effulgent appetites—perhaps I should put "appalled" in quotation marks, given the hypocrisy of their dismay (especially when it came to adultery, which, during the Clinton years, proved a pastime that merrily transcended partisan boundaries). To judge from Clinton's consistently high approval ratings in the polls, the public was more tolerant—and, perhaps, secretly enjoyed—these unruly passions.

I'D FIRST MET BILL CLINTON at a meeting of the Democratic Leadership Council in Philadelphia, in 1989. We were introduced by Al From, the president of the DLC, who hooked a thumb in Clinton's direction and said, "This guy delivers our message better than any other politician."

The Democratic Leadership Council had been formed in 1985, as a moderate, mostly Southern response to the leftward rush—and attendant electoral failures—of the Democratic Party since the 1960s. There was a fair amount of skepticism among mainstream (read: liberal) Democrats about the DLC, whose early meetings were notable mostly for the number of corporate lobbyists in attendance. The group was derided as the "Southern White Boys," or, in Jesse Jackson's phrase, "Democrats for the Leisure Class." The inference was that these were Democrats who were uncomfortable with the politically inconvenient, but profoundly moral, decision their party had made to embrace the civil rights and antiwar movements in the 1960s, a time when the Republicans had successfully—and not very subtly—launched a "Southern strategy" designed to cultivate the region's white majority. (As a result, the Democrats had lost the South in every presidential election since 1964—except for Jimmy Carter's 1976 victory—and, with the advent of Ronald Reagan, they had begun to lose the white, blue-collar vote in the rest of the country as well.)

By the mid-1980s, the Democrats seemed permanently boggled. The moderates in the party were held hostage by a cornucopia of special interest groups (feminists, minorities, environmentalists, trade unionists) who seemed more concerned with the purity of their causes than with winning elections. There was an intellectual sclerosis as well. The most vocal activists on the left tended to blame "society"—which really meant the free market system—for the rapidly rising crime rate and for a relatively new, stubbornly persistent form of intergenerational poverty, which was marked by out-of-wedlock births and welfare dependency. Indeed, many liberal Democrats refused to acknowledge—or worse, dismissed as "racist"—the tidal wave of sociological research that proved, as Daniel Patrick Moynihan had first observed in 1965, that the disintegration of the two-parent family in poor African-American neighborhoods was having vast social consequences: that children born to single mothers were far more likely to drop out of school, to use drugs, to commit crimes, and to become single parents themselves than were children born into households where a father and mother were both present. Anyone who suggested that poor people might have a better chance to succeed if they behaved more responsibly was said to be "blaming the victim." At its worst, this witless, reflexive, and utterly condescending tendency held the poor to a lower standard of morality than the rest of society and expanded the definition of "victimhood" to include most criminals.

The Democrats also suffered from a near-absolute belief in the immorality of almost every sort of American military activity abroad in the post-Vietnam era, from the placing of Pershing missiles in Europe to various (in fairness, almost always dubious and very often criminal) crusades against indigenous villains in Latin America to the prosecution of the Gulf War. And finally, at a time when government had lost credibility and was beset by enormous budget deficits, the Democrats were, proudly, the party of government. The largest, most powerful factions in the party were the public employees unions, particularly the teachers unions (who had come to represent the single largest bloc of delegates at the quadrennial Democratic Party nominating convention). "We're the party of teachers," a frustrated Al From said at the end of the futile Dukakis campaign for the presidency in 1988, "when we should be the party of education."

And so, there came to be a yearning among many Democrats, even non-Southerners, for a less precious party. Traditional liberalism seemed stale, elitist, and, in many of its social and foreign policy nostrums, just plain wrong. The conservatives, who had built vast think tanks like the Heritage Foundation and the American Enterprise Institute, were quicker, fresher, and more confident in debate; often, they seemed more interested in new ideas than the Democrats did (the Heritage Foundation, for example, had developed an ideologically counterintuitive proposal for universal health insurance—a voucher plan funded by a progressive tax on wealthier Americans) Al From was jealous. He believed that the only way to reinvigorate the Democratic Party was to reinvent liberalism; he was very much in the market for new ideas and new leaders. He longed for a Heritage-style operation and, in 1989, the Democratic Leadership Council launched a small think tank called the Progressive Policy Institute (PPI). This turned out to be From's second most important initiative that year: The first was to recruit Bill Clinton to become the chairman of the DLC.

In April 1989, From went to Little Rock and offered Clinton the job. There followed a halting, anguished mating ritual of the sort that has now become Bill Clinton's signature in both life and politics. The governor seemed to love the idea, but . . . he didn't quite accept the post. Months passed and From grew impatient. He saw Clinton again in the autumn and then again at the National Governors Conference in February 1990. There was still no firm commitment. "What's going on?" From fumed. "You said you were going to do it. Well, are you or aren't you?"

"I've got a big decision to make," Clinton told him. "I've got to decide whether I'm going to run for governor again. If I don't do it, I'm going to have to figure out some way to make $100,000 a year to support my family."

"I said to him, 'You stupid son-of-a-bitch, I'll pay you $100,000 right now to be chairman of the DLC,' " From later recalled, with a laugh. "That's why I never believed he was money-corrupt during the Whitewater business—the guy had no sense of his own worth."

In time, Clinton chose to do both: He ran for reelection as governor and became chairman of the DLC (without pay). But one sensed a reluctance on Clinton's part to identify himself so closely with one wing of the Democratic Party; his ties to the liberals were older, and just as deep—he'd run Texas for George McGovern's presidential campaign in 1972 and he included old friends like the liberal political scientist, Robert Reich, then of Harvard, and Marion Wright Edelman of the Children's Defense Fund, among his closest advisors. McGovern himself went so far, early in the 1992 campaign, as to describe the Clinton's New Democratic project as a liberal "Trojan horse."

But Reich would eventually arrive at a more nuanced conclusion: "Bill Clinton operates by sonar. He emits a huge number of policies, ideas, and initiatives and he sees what kind of response he gets. And where he sees an opportunity to move, he moves."

The implication was a value-free pragmatism, and there was a fair amount of evidence to validate Reich's bitter judgment. The President often said he had come to Washington to "*do* things" or to "get things done"—a formulation vague enough to discomfort almost everyone. A pattern emerged in the 1992 campaign and continued through his presidency: Clinton would initially succeed as a moderate, then he would try to move left and plummet, then he would shuffle back to the center again. In the political sonar of the 1990s, the resonance was all in the middle, which led Clinton's moderate supporters to wonder obsessively why he so frequently succumbed to the temptation to move left. Was he a closet liberal? Or was he just a pragmatist who understood that the political calculus often demanded that he keep the party stalwarts happy? Or were there other, darker pressures—from his wife, from the people who raised money for the party, from the Hollywood sorts whose company he so clearly enjoyed?

Of course, few successful politicians manage to remain ideologically pure for very long, even when the "ideology" in question is opportunistic pragmatism. The most basic rule of politics is: You have to pacify your party's fanatics ("securing the base" is the term of art). Clinton could not have won the nomination in 1992, or survived his first term (or impeachment, for that matter), if he hadn't kept the most devoted Democrats happy. And the most devoted Democrats not only remained liberal, but pompously so, vestigially convinced of the righteousness of European-style social democracy: The New Democrat philosophy was seen—and is *still* seen by die-hard, old-style lefties—as a cynical corruption of the true faith, an electoral strategy gussied up as a political philosophy. Which was rather ironic, since traditional liberals soon began to adopt many of the positions that the Progressive Policy Institute had developed in the early 1990s (the importance of fiscal conservatism, a greater insistence on responsible social behavior, and a more aggressive posture in the world, to name three). Still, even Al From would have moments when he would wonder if Bill Clinton had hooked up with the New Democrats merely because their message polled so well. "That's true," From says, "but from the start, Bill Clinton was always with us on the issues, especially big ones like day care."

ALTHOUGH THE BATTLE OVER DAY care assistance is remembered now only by the most hopeless of policy wonks, it represented, in the late 1980s, the purest example of the philosophical difference between Old and New Democrats—and it remained, until Hillary Clinton began her campaign for the United States Senate, the only policy issue on which the First Lady took a position sharply opposed to that of her husband. Mrs. Clinton stood with her friend Marion Wright Edelman of the Children's Defense Fund and with most congressional Democrats in support of the ABC Bill, a classic piece of liberal legislation that would have funded state-supervised day care centers for the working poor throughout the nation with licensed operators and guaranteed standards. Traditional conservatives scoffed at this, calling it "government baby-sitting." They opposed any and all day care funding. These two positions, and the gulf between them, were a splendid demonstration of the prevailing aridity of public policy debate.

Enter the National Governors Association, which, in itself, was a highly unusual occurrence. The governors rarely inserted themselves, as a group, into federal legislative debates—in part because the standing rule of their organization was that any official policy position had to be approved *unanimously* by all fifty governors. In this case, however, Bill Clinton and his Republican colleague, Tom Kean of New Jersey, a Republican, had found a path between the liberal and conservative positions—a Third Way, to coin a phrase—and they had managed to secure the support of all their peers. They proposed a tax credit (in effect, a voucher) that would go directly to poor people in need of day care, empowering them to spend the money wherever they wanted. This was a felicitous solution that, in one stroke, provided the poor with day care assistance (which liberals were demanding) via a form of tax reduction (which conservatives certainly couldn't oppose).

This formula—liberal ends through conservative means—was at the very heart of The Third Way. The day care debate launched a furiously creative period in domestic policy-making. The Progressive Policy Institute opened in late 1989 and challenged Democratic Party orthodoxy in its very first position paper: an argument *against* a higher minimum wage and in favor of an expanded Earned Income Tax Credit (the latter, a reverse income tax, gave money directly to the working poor—it was similar to the day care tax credit). Many of the ideas that Bill Clinton would run on and then try to implement—from welfare reform to national service to a voucherized job-training system—were promoted by the PPI during this period.

Indeed, a delightfully dangerous centrist radicalism was in the air. The political spectrum seemed, suddenly, an arrow—with moderates pointing the way to the future and the traditional left and right wings lagging behind, hopelessly retro. The academics who populated PPI were open to any and all creative heresies— even the ultimate heresy: communing with Republicans. A series of monthly dinners was soon organized by a PPI fellow named Elaine Kamarck (who later became Al Gore's domestic policy director) and by Jim Pinkerton, a junior domestic policy advisor in the White House who seemed to be working the same intellectual turf as the New Democrats and was routinely ignored by President Bush; most of the senior PPI fellows and Al From attended, as did stray members of the press (*mea culpa*) and assorted Republicans, particularly Libertarians (Newt Gingrich never missed a meal).

Much of the discussion at these dinners, which Pinkerton puckishly called "The New Paradigm Society," started from the notion, made popular by the pop-futurists Alvin and Heidi Toffler, that, while the Industrial Age "paradigm" had been marked by centralized structures like bureaucracies and assembly lines, the new economy would be decentralized, interactive—built like a computer network—and government would have to adapt to this new world. "The two things we learned in the eighties were entirely contradictory," Pinkerton would often say. "Socialism doesn't work, and the most ideological President of the twentieth century, Ronald Reagan, couldn't put an end to the welfare state. He couldn't even put a dent in it."

Thus, the job of the radical centrists was to create a welfare state for the Information Age, one that acknowledged that government was necessary but might act less obtrusively if it took advantage of the efficiencies that came with markets. Centralized, bureaucratic solutions were too ponderous to succeed in the new economy—that had been the most important lesson learned by American corporations in the 1980s, and the thinkers associated with the Progressive Policy Institute believed this principle needed to be applied to the public sector now. Competition was good; accountability was essential; programs had to be free to fail. The same parameters could be applied to almost any area of government activity—from education to health care to old-age pensions to sanitation.

Clinton was more cautious than the wonks in his advocacy of The New Whatever. But, oh, could he talk policy! He seemed to know more about the school choice experiment in East Harlem than the governor of New York did; he knew all about the competitive bidding for sanitation contracts in Phoenix, the public housing manager in Omaha who'd come up with a great after-school program for the kids in the projects, the terrific for-profit welfare-to-work program in New York. One of the first times I traveled with Clinton, I asked if he'd heard that David Osborne was about to coauthor a new book about local reform movements across the country with the catchy title *Reinventing Government*.

"Read the galleys." He sniffed, apparently disappointed that I wasn't so far along in my reading as he was. "Great stuff."

But Clinton also understood the meaner calculations a Democrat would have to make if he wanted to be elected president. He would have to seem tougher on crime than Michael Dukakis had, especially on the squalid, and substantially irrelevant, issue of the death penalty (indeed, Clinton would approve the execution of a mentally retarded black man, Ricky Ray Rector, in the midst of the presidential campaign). He would have to be something more than a pacifist when it came to foreign policy (although Clinton's position on the Senate's vote to authorize the Gulf War had been a hilarious fudge: "I guess I would have voted with the majority if it was a close vote, but I agree with the arguments of the minority"). He would have to traverse a narrow passage on social issues (pro gay rights but against gay marriage; pro affirmative action but against racial quotas). He would have to seem more concerned with the problems of the "forgotten" middle class than with those of the poor. Some of these were uncomfortable for Clinton, but they were part of the price to be paid for political credibility—and easily justified by the most ancient political principle: If elected, Clinton would be more sensitive on all these issues than the incumbent President was.

Clinton had put these disparate intellectual, policy, and political pieces into place by the time that the Democratic Leadership Council held its annual convention in Cleveland in early May 1991. A bland processional of Democratic hopefuls—Al Gore, Richard Gephardt, and Jay Rockefeller, among others—was scheduled to appear; a large national press contingent was there to rate the contestants. Clinton was last to speak.

He did not have a prepared text, but improvised from twenty-one single word cues he'd scrawled on a piece of paper. He began with a recitation of the alleged problems of the "forgotten" middle class and then he said:

"You may say . . . Why in the world haven't the Democrats been able to take advantage of these conditions?

"I'll tell you why: because too many of the people who used to vote for us, the very burdened middle class we are talking about, have not trusted us in national elections to defend our national interests abroad, to put their values into our social policy at home, or to take their tax money and spend it with discipline."

And then he uttered a now-famous mantra for the first time: "Our burden is to give the people a new choice, rooted in old values, a new choice that is simple, that offers *opportunity*, demands *responsibility*, gives citizens more say, provides them with responsive government—all because we recognize that we are a *community*. We are all in this together, and we are going up and down together."

Al From had never heard the message synthesized so perfectly before. The press proclaimed Clinton the best of the Cleveland orators. In every possible way—substantively, politically, oratorically—this was one of the most important speeches of Clinton's career. But Mario Cuomo, the governor of New York and a no-show in Cleveland, was still the presumed front-runner for the Democratic nomination, and President George Bush was still enjoying historic levels of popularity after his Gulf War victory. Even after the Cleveland triumph, the presidency of the United States must have seemed a very distant prospect for Bill Clinton. Two days after the speech—on May 8, 1991—he was back in Little Rock, attending an industrial promotion meeting at a local hotel. A state employee working at one of the booths caught his eye. According to subsequent testimony, the governor of Arkansas asked a state trooper named Danny Ferguson to see if the young woman would be willing to meet privately upstairs. The woman, whose name was Paula Corbin Jones, said she would be delighted to meet with the governor.

IT WAS ONE THING TO hear Bill Clinton talk about policy; it was quite another to watch him actually campaign for the presidency. There was a physical, almost carnal, quality to his public appearances. He embraced audiences and was aroused by them in turn. His sonar was remarkable in retail political situations. He seemed able to sense what audiences needed and deliver it to them—trimming his pitch here, emphasizing different priorities there, always aiming to please. This was one of his most effective, and maddening, qualities in private meetings as well: He always grabbed on to some point of agreement, while steering the conversation away from larger points of disagreement—leaving his seducee with the distinct impression that they were in total harmony on just about everything. (Once, early in the campaign, he sat quietly as his aide Harold Ickes and I had a furious argument about the social utility of public employees unions. When it was over, he shook my hand, looked me in the eye, and said, with deep and obvious conviction, "Joe, I want you to know, I *always* value your opinion.")

There was a needy, high-cholesterol quality to it all; the public seemed enthralled by his vast, messy humanity. Try as he might to keep in shape, jogging for miles with his pale thighs jiggling, he still tended toward a raw pink fleshiness. He was famously addicted to junk food. He had a reputation as a womanizer. All these were of a piece. Indeed, the news that he'd been fooling around with an Arkansas lounge singer named Gennifer Flowers, which appeared in a supermarket tabloid a few weeks before the New Hampshire primary, almost seemed redundant. It was

---

only when that peccadillo was compounded by a second, more serious scandal—he was caught lying about his determined efforts to avoid the military draft during the war in Vietnam—that his poll numbers began to drop. Even then, the damage was temporary.

On the night before the New Hampshire primary, well after his last scheduled public appearance, I found Clinton going from table to table at a local restaurant, shaking hands, chatting with anyone willing to engage him. He went from restaurant to restaurant through the dinner hour, and then made a tour of the bowling alleys of Manchester—until just past midnight, when there were no more hands to shake, no more places to go except back to his hotel. He was exhausted and flu-ridden; his face was flushed, his eyes were red and bleary, but he wasn't quite ready to pack it in. "You want to bowl a game?" he asked me.

If I remember correctly, Clinton bowled in his stocking feet, his white shirttail hanging out. At times, as we stood there, waiting for our balls to return down the alley, he'd lean up against me—a strange feline sensation; he needed the physical contact.

THE CLINTON CAMPAIGN APPEARED TO exist entirely, and very comfortably, within the grammar of popular culture—a cross between a disaster movie and a country music song. The governor roused his languishing campaign by playing the saxophone on Arsenio Hall's television program; he distanced himself from Jesse Jackson by attacking a rap singer named Sister Souljah; his wife compared herself to Tammy Wynette. He traveled by bus. His staff called him Elvis—and, more privately, "The Natural," after the character played by Robert Redford in the film adaptation of Bernard Malamud's baseball novel. He was, the consultant Paul Begala would say quoting the film, "the best there ever was." It was all great fun, and the distant, patrician President George Bush provided a perfect foil.

But there was also a touching, uncynical transparency to the campaign: The candidate actually seemed moved by the stories he heard along the way, and the stories, more often than not, fit his vision of the challenge ahead. People—factory workers, middle managers, the folks who populated the fast-food restaurants he visited—really were scared about the future: Would there be a place for *them* in the new, high-tech global economy? James Carville's famous sign—"It's the economy, stupid"—was posted to keep the campaign staff "on message." The candidate himself needed no such reminders.

The campaign reached its climax in the second presidential debate on October 15, 1992, in Richmond, Virginia—a town meeting that included spontaneous questions from the audience. The candidates sat on high stools, were given wireless mikes and were free to wander about the stage. Toward the end of the debate, an African-American woman asked a confusing question: "How has the national debt personally affected each of your lives? And if it hasn't, how can you honestly find a cure for the economic problems of the common people if you have no experience in what's ailing them?"

Bush: "I'm sure it has. I love my grandchildren. I'm not sure I get . . . help me with the question."

Q: "Well, I've had friends who've been laid off from their jobs."

Moderator: "I think she means the recession . . . rather than the deficit."

Bush: "Well, listen, you ought to be in the White House for a day and hear what I hear . . . I was in the Lomax AME Church. It's a black church just outside Washington, D.C. And I read the bulletin about teenage pregnancies, about the difficulties people are having making ends meet . . ."

After more such struggle, it was Clinton's turn—and he did something quite extraordinary. He took three steps toward the woman and asked her, "Tell me how it's affected you again?"

The woman was speechless. Clinton helped her along, describing some of the terrible economic stories he'd heard as governor of Arkansas. But the words weren't as important as the body language: The three steps he had taken toward the woman spoke volumes about his empathy, his concern, his desire to respond to the needs of the public. Bush, by contrast, was caught gazing at his wristwatch—hoping desperately that this awkward moment would soon be done.

And, indeed, it was: The presidential campaign was, in effect, over.

CHAPTER
TWO

In his first television interview after the election, Bill Clinton told Ted Koppel of ABC that he was going to "focus on the economy like a laser beam." The economy did become his priority, but the public saw a rather different picture during his first six months in office: mayhem, disorder, a sudden emphasis on obscure issues (like gays in the military), and personal quirks (rumors of pitched battles between the Clintons, tussles with the permanent White House domestic staff)—in short, amateur hour.

Clinton's transition from candidate to President is considered by many historians, and by more than a few staff members who suffered through it, as the worst in modern history. He was exhausted from the campaign, but refused to take a vacation—and, in his very first press conference as President-elect, on November 11, 1991, he made a serious mistake. Asked if he would stand by his pledge to allow homosexuals to serve openly in the military, Clinton said yes. The military issue had never been very important to the homosexual activist groups, who were more concerned with equal protection on the job, with marriage and partnership rights, and with funding for AIDS research; oddly, the Republicans had chosen not to highlight this lesser Clinton pledge during the campaign. And a more alert President-elect could easily have slipped past the question. (The classic Clintonian response would have been: "Yes, we're going to ask the military to study the situation and come up with a plan"—to be implemented sometime in the next century.)

"It sent precisely the wrong message," said one of Clinton's campaign advisors. "I'm not saying he shouldn't have taken that position. But as the first thing he did? It was exactly the sort of 'liberal elitist' issue that we'd been trying to submerge throughout the campaign. It sent the signal that he was going to govern differently from the way he campaigned—as an 'Old' Democrat."

This was also the first glimmer of what would become a significant problem during the Clinton years: his administration's uncertainty about—and unfamiliarity with—the military. "This was simply not something that Democrats thought about very much during their long years out of power," said Larry K. Smith, a defense policy analyst who served as counselor to Clinton's first two Secretaries of Defense. "The culture of the military was foreign to them. Careful consideration of how to use force simply wasn't in their DNA."

Other disturbing signals followed. Clinton spent most of November and December fitting together a jigsaw Cabinet that "looked like America," perfectly balanced—at least, according to traditional liberal perceptions—along racial, ethnic, and gender lines. This was silly on several counts. In the modern presidency, the real power resides with those closest to the President—the White House staff. All but a few Cabinet members are peripheral. Clinton seemed more preoccupied with the need for a second Hispanic (Denver mayor Federico Peña, who was considered less than brilliant by Clinton's aides, displaced the estimable Chicago pol William Daley as Transportation Secretary at the last moment) and with the search for a woman Attorney General than with working out a coherent management structure for the West Wing. (The latter dragnet, a hapless burlesque managed by the First Lady, did eventually turn up a stubborn, mystifying, often naïve, and only occasionally loyal Old Democrat named Janet Reno, who lingered through all eight years, even though Clinton later admitted that she was his least favorite Cabinet member.) A week before the inauguration, there were members of the eventual inner circle of advisors who hadn't been told what their jobs would be. It would be two years before the White House was truly put in order.

The first chief of staff, a friend of Clinton's since kindergarten named Thomas (Mac) McLarty, was a modest, moderate sort who was completely inexperienced in the ways of Washington and quite unprepared for the crisis-a-minute intensity of the presidency. In fact, McLarty had warned Clinton that it might be wiser to find a chief of staff who had actually served in the White House before. That, however, was easier said than done. It had been twelve years since the last Democratic President, and Jimmy Carter's defiantly apolitical White House stood, in Clinton's mind, as the perfect model of administrative incompetence. Still, there *were* clever Democrats about, people who understood the complex rhythms and metabolism of the capital. But the Clintons—and Hillary clearly played a significant role in staff selection—wore their predisposition against the local talent (who, in fairness, tend to be a preening, inbred, nearsighted lot) as a badge of honor. Of course, when it comes to building a staff, most presidents have a weakness for friends and family; the Clintons had been involved in frantic, meritocratic Rolodex-building ever since Yale Law School. But their search for the Best and Brightest Baby Boomers had an important caveat: They were particularly attracted to those who were slavish, unobtrusive, and loyal; forceful personalities were not courted, Washington dinner party regulars were shunned—anyone who might be less than worshipful was considered suspect, a probable source of news leaks, a potential enemy. This is a quality common to most high-powered politicians, but it was strange to find it so pronounced in people as strong and intelligent—and as open to philosophical dispute—as the Clintons were.

As a result, some of the most clever and experienced Democratic Party operatives found themselves shut out of the Administration or marginalized—people like Mike McCurry and Tom Donilon (both of whom found a home at the State Department); Richard Holbrooke, arguably the most skillful diplomat in the party; as well as New Democrat policy experts like Elaine Kamarck and the economist Robert Shapiro. Some, like McCurry and Holbrooke, eventually played important roles, but it must be said that Clinton's staff was never particularly strong (or very discreet, for that matter). "There was always the sense," said a prominent Democrat, "that Bill and Hillary thought they could do it all themselves."

There was, however, one aspect of the early Clinton operation that was entirely professional: the work on an economic plan of action, particularly the formulation of the President's first budget, which would have to be presented almost immediately after the election. Clinton *had* taken the economy more seriously than any other issue in the campaign. He had assembled a team of six advisors. Three of them—Bob Rubin and Roger Altman, who were investment bankers, plus Rob Shapiro of the Progressive Policy Institute—were "deficit hawks," who believed that if the incredible annual budget deficits of the Reagan–Bush era (estimated to be over $300 billion in Clinton's first year in office) could be brought under control, interest rates would be reduced and the economy would begin to grow again. The other three advisors—Robert Reich, Ira Magaziner, and Derek Shearer—were old Clinton pals who tended to be more liberal and academic. They grudgingly agreed that deficit reduction was important, but they placed more emphasis on encouraging economic growth through "investment" (which had become the prevailing euphemism for government spending) in education, social services, and other traditional liberal public works.

The first year of the Clinton budget-making process would become the subject of a book by Bob Woodward called *The Agenda*, which was remarkable for its detailed accounting of the endless and seemingly chaotic meetings within the White House. But many of the central characters believe that Woodward's account, while accurate in its details, was skewed toward melodrama and underestimated the resolute quality of the operation. A famous Woodward anecdote had the President wailing that he was going to be remembered as an Eisenhower Republican (this was accurate, a lovely detail, but little more than a stray moment of frustration in a process that resulted in an extremely purposeful, and arguably courageous, economic scheme).

The President did bellow and thrash—his temper was shocking to those who didn't know him well—and his frustration over the straitened budgetary circumstances was real, but the outcome of the internal debate was never in doubt. Clinton's first personnel selections during the transition made clear which side he was on: He asked the conservative Texas senator Lloyd Bentsen to be Treasury Secretary, and Leon Panetta of California, chairman of the House Budget Committee, to run the Office of Management and Budget; and he created a new structure—the National Economic Council, which would be led by Rubin—to coordinate the various, intricate aspects of economic policy. All three men were deficit hawks. "He believed from the start that deficit reduction was the predicate, that we couldn't have a credible activist government unless we could get the budget under control," Hillary Clinton later told me. "I compare it to the importance of education in Arkansas. We couldn't get the economy moving there unless more people had the skills necessary for better jobs. In 1993, our most important job was dealing with 'Stockman's Revenge'—which I think was Daniel Patrick Moynihan's term for the massive deficits that the Reagan tax cuts and defense buildup had created. Unless we dealt with the deficits first," Mrs. Clinton concluded, "we'd never be able to do any of the other things we wanted to do." (Robert Reich, who led the economic team through the transition process and then was shuttled off to the Labor Department, called the debilitating impact of the Republican budget deficits, first imagined by Reagan budget director David Stockman, "the law of intended consequences"—in other words, the Reagan tax cut was *intended* to produce budget deficits that would prevent new federal programs.

The deficit-hawk route was, however, a risky course of action based on unproven economic theory. It was "known"—mysteriously, but conclusively—that Alan Greenspan, the Federal Reserve chairman, would only consider "credible" a package that included $500 billion of deficit reduction, projected over five years; without the $500 billion, Greenspan was likely to keep interest rates high. But why $500 billion, as opposed to $375 billion? And what if the economy didn't respond to the reduced interest rates? Indeed, classical Keynesian liberals could, and did, argue that this sort of reduction in government spending might push the economy—just then emerging from a mild recession—into another tailspin. But Clinton had made his choice. "I believed there were vast flows of venture capital—confidence capital—that were out there bursting and waiting to happen," the President told me later. "There was a vast, pent-up potential in the American economy . . . and [I knew that] if I didn't get the economy going, nothing else would matter in the end."

Clinton's new economic team—most of whom were strangers to him—was pleasantly surprised by the President's willingness to take this monumental political risk, and by his ability to assimilate complicated macroeconomic concepts, but the First Lady wasn't: "In law school, Bill did a typical Bill thing in his

Corporate Finance class," she recalled. "He never went to lectures, but then he spent a week or two cramming, and he got the highest grade in the class. The professor called him, a bit miffed I believe, and asked how it was possible that he was able to do so well. 'It's just like politics,' Bill said. 'All you have to figure out is who's screwing who.' "

Indeed, the Clinton economic team was facing two hurdles that no one had predicted. First, the actual deficit numbers were extraordinarily dismal (which was part of the reason for Greenspan's $500 billion demand). Within days after the election, the Government Accounting Office announced that the deficit would be $300 billion larger than expected. Clinton had said throughout the campaign that he intended to increase taxes on the wealthy, but now it was becoming apparent that he also would have to "delay" many of the programs he had promised, including the middle-class tax cut—and that he would have to continue the Bush administration's policy of painful spending "caps" on all domestic programs except the so-called entitlements like Social Security and Medicare, where higher spending levels were mandated by law. These developments were particularly distressing to Clinton's old campaign consultants—James Carville, Paul Begala, Mandy Grunwald, and the pollster Stan Greenberg—who were not official members of the White House staff, but who remained deeply involved in the "message" operation (the fact that they carried White House access passes, even though they weren't official staff members, was one of the sillier controversies that found its way into the press early on). The consultants, not surprisingly, tended to be militant believers in what worked politically: They were social conservatives (tough on crime, in favor of welfare reform, allergic to lifestyle issues like gays in the military) but they were also considerably more liberal on economic questions than were the deficit hawks—and they were fearful that Clinton was in the process of forgetting why he'd been elected President. "George Bush had just lost the presidency because he had broken his 'no new taxes' pledge," Mandy Grunwald recalled, "and there we were, breaking our promise to have a middle-class tax cut—and not doing nearly as much 'investment' as he had promised, either."

The consultants' argument was emotionally powerful and it made sense politically—and it was bolstered by the second unexpected hurdle that the economic plan faced: Clinton and the congressional Democrats would have to get his straitened, conservative, "Eisenhower" budget passed without *any* help from the opposition party.

Not a single Republican would vote for the Clinton economic plan. Leon Panetta learned this early in 1993, when he had a conversation with his old friend Senator Pete Domenici of New Mexico, the ranking Republican on the Senate Budget Committee. "Leon," Domenici said, "we've been told by the leadership that we just can't support anything with a tax increase in it."

Clinton was astonished when Panetta reported the news. They couldn't even hope for the votes of moderate senators like John Chafee of Rhode Island or Jim Jeffords of Vermont? he asked. No, Mr. President, Panetta replied. Worse, there were more than a few Democrats who were itching to jump ship as well—particularly those from oil and gas states who were opposed to new energy taxes (the original Clinton plan included a worthy but too-complicated tax, suggested by Vice President

Al Gore, on British thermal units, or Btu's, which is a standard measurement of energy use). And so, early on—within weeks of his inauguration—it was apparent that the budget battle would be far more grueling than anyone had anticipated. It loomed as a terrible, draining struggle that was likely to cripple almost everything else Clinton was hoping to accomplish in his first year.

It was also apparent, from the start, that Bill Clinton would not be granted the traditional presidential "honeymoon" by either the media or the Republicans. Quite the opposite, in fact. His presidency would mark an unprecedented escalation in the levels of partisan enmity and journalistic fecklessness in Washington. "Maybe there were things I could have done" to ameliorate the atmosphere, Clinton lamented years later. And there was some truth to that. He might have reached out more aggressively to the congressional Republican leaders, Senator Bob Dole and Congressman Bob Michel, both moderates with a history of finding ways to compromise with the opposition. He might also have been a bit less solicitous toward the Democratic leaders, Senate Majority Leader George Mitchell and House Speaker Tom Foley, whom he'd invited to Little Rock for dinner within days after the election (along with the antique, but powerful, Senator Robert Byrd of West Virginia). The congressional Democrats, whose majorities had given them great power over a long line of Republican presidents, demanded obeisance—they weren't pleased with the reform agenda that Clinton had proposed as a candidate—smaller congressional staffs, a line-item veto, campaign finance reform—and the new President acceded, sending an initial, debilitating signal of weakness. "Clinton was very aware of what happened to Jimmy Carter, who alienated the Democratic congressional leaders early on and paid an enormous price for it," said Al From. "He was going to need Mitchell and Foley to get his program through, and that gave them a lot of leverage. Another lesson from Jimmy Carter was if you allow yourself to be challenged from the left—as Carter did, by Ted Kennedy—the result is disaster."

In truth, though, there wasn't much that Bill Clinton could do about the looming political bloodbath. The Republicans had not controlled the House of Representatives in nearly forty years, and there was a new generation of radicals, led by Newt Gingrich, who were intending to be as tough on this new Democratic President as the Democrats had been on Nixon and Reagan. Even Bob Dole, whom Gingrich had once called "the tax collector for the welfare state," felt heat from his right: His initial response to Clinton's election victory was remarkably ungracious—he said he was going to represent the 57 percent of the electorate who'd voted against the new President. "I guess I was pretty upset," Dole told me later. "But if you could bring prosperity back by raising taxes, why hadn't anybody thought of it before?"

The result was that the new President found himself working with the narrowest of margins in his effort to pass his 1993 budget. It had been expected to pass the House easily—since the Democrats held a 257-to-177-seat majority—but it passed by only a single vote. And the Senate would be even more difficult, the political equivalent of trench warfare; individual senators had the power to kidnap the entire plan. David Boren of Oklahoma would not accept a Btu tax, so a four-cent gasoline tax replaced it (and Boren still voted against the plan); Bob Kerrey of Nebraska was infuriated by Clinton's unwillingness to address the rising cost of entitlements like Social Security and Medicare—he was placated at the last moment by the promise of a commission to study entitlement reform and he provided the last vote necessary for passage of the budget.

As a result of these tactical retreats, Clinton soon gained the reputation—in Washington, at least—of being a weak President, one who could be rolled. His decision to abandon the Btu tax, after a great many House Democrats had cast politically difficult votes for it, did immediate damage to his reputation in Congress. The notion that Clinton had no "core values" was becoming a Beltway cliché. And yet, most of the people who participated in the endless internal meetings about the budget plan were aware that there had been lines that Clinton wouldn't cross, promises he wouldn't abandon. Two of his campaign proposals, both distinctively New Democrat ideas, were sacrosanct. He insisted upon the establishment of AmeriCorps, the national service program that had been the best applause line of his presidential campaign. And, more important, he insisted on a massive expansion of the Earned Income Tax Credit—another applause line from the campaign: "No one should have to work forty hours a week and raise a family in poverty."

The decision to grant a significant increase in the EITC was a crucial, if little noticed, moment in the presidency. Lloyd Bentsen noted that the proposed gasoline tax increase could be eliminated if the President agreed to scale back the EITC. If Clinton insisted on taxing Americans' most vehemently precious right—the happy pursuit of world petroleum resources at ridiculously low prices—a great many Southern Democrats would jump ship, and a great many Republicans would question both the President's patriotism and sanity. The opposition would be able to say, "Not only did he lie about a tax cut, he *raised* taxes on the middle class." So the political benefits of dropping the gas tax were obvious. And there was *no* political benefit to expanding the Earned Income Tax Credit. No one would notice if the prospective recipients—the legions of waitresses, hospital orderlies, and janitors—still toiled for wages that left them below the poverty line; the EITC subsidy was too cumbersome a concept for most journalists to even bother to understand, much less attempt to describe.

Bentsen was the most senior, and most respected, man in the room during the budget deliberations—but he was opposed by George Stephanopoulos and by Gene Sperling, a diminutive and very junior but extremely devoted economic aide. At one point, the unlikely sparring between Sperling and Bentsen became so intense that Roger Altman, the deputy Treasury Secretary, said, "Why don't we let Gene and Lloyd take it outside?"

"Because," the President said with a laugh, "pretty soon folks would be saying, 'Whatever happened to old Gene?' "

But Clinton sided with old Gene. He expanded the Earned Income Tax Credit from $15.9 to $21.2 billion in the first year, which, in effect, cut taxes for fifteen million families. "Here we were, all these brilliant spinners," Stephanopoulos said later, "and none of us figured out, until months later, that we had actually *passed* the middle-class tax cut: It was the Earned Income Tax Credit." (This may have been a belated Stephanopoulos spin: Others say that a conscious decision was made not to publicize the EITC expansion, since the forgotten middle class might resent the beneficence bestowed upon the working poor.)

POLITICIANS DON'T LIKE abstractions. They want tangible accomplishments: roads built, taxes cut, jobs created. Presidents, in particular, like to start a new administration with a big, solid legislative victory—the conventional wisdom is that the first year in office is your best chance to impose your will upon the Congress. Bill Clinton had bet his future on the abstraction of smaller deficits. There is the temptation, given the ultimate success of the policy, to undervalue the courage of that decision now. A less earnest, more cynical politician might have behaved differently, might have tried to make himself popular, as his successor did, by proposing a big tax cut or the old-fashioned liberal spending program that many Democrats were encouraging him to offer. (Clinton did make a futile, half-hearted effort to enact a small economic stimulus package, which died quickly and ignominiously in the Senate. "I thought of it as our insurance policy," said Gene Sperling. "It never would have been large enough to make an impact, but when the stimulus plan died we were left with the pain of reduced spending as our only 'accomplishment.' We had staked everything on the theory that lower deficits would lead to lower interests rates, which would revive the economy—which, you have to remember, was an *unproven* theory at that point.")

Soon Clinton would spend even more political capital on another abstraction: the promise of free trade. He would campaign that autumn for the North American Free Trade Agreement (NAFTA), which had been negotiated by his Republican predecessor and was vehemently opposed by a majority of the Democratic House members who had just taken a political risk to support his budget plan. (Indeed, Marjorie Margolies-Mezvinsky of Pennsylvania, who cast the deciding vote on the budget in the House, would be defeated for reelection by a Republican who never tired of reminding voters that the incumbent had voted for "higher taxes.")

By any fair accounting, Bill Clinton was running a very serious presidency—and yet his administration, as portrayed in the media and perceived by the political community in Washington, seemed trivial, juvenile, a circus. Both the President and Mrs. Clinton quickly developed reputations for being self-centered, high-handed, and strangely secretive. Relations with the press were awful from the start. The First Lady, in particular, was intent on keeping reporters as distant as possible—at first, she tried to cast them out of the White House entirely, proposing that the press room be relocated across the alley, in the Old Executive Office Building. Failing that, an attempt was made to keep the door between the press secretary's office and the press room closed—which also failed. There was a dunderheaded but successful effort, also involving the First Lady, to replace the entrenched Travel Office staff with Arkansas friends. (This was pretty much politics as usual, but for one crucial factor: The Travel Office regulars had provided perks and favors—like free transport of purchases made during overseas presidential trips—for the White House press corps for many years and had earned the reciprocal loyalty of the pack.) And then, there were the occasional imperial tics: At one point, it was reported (and much later found to be untrue) that the President had stymied traffic at Los Angeles International Airport by getting a haircut from the noted Hollywood barber, Christo, while Air Force One was parked on the runway. There were also some juicy rumors emanating from the residence—if true, they could only have been retailed by the Secret Service or by the permanent White House domestic staff. A story that the First Lady had tossed a lamp at the President gained wide, if unsubstantiated, currency. This was the sort of news that dominated the early months of the Clinton presidency.

The internal mayhem at the White House was soon legendary: The public image was of callow, arrogant aides wandering about in dungarees, pulling unnecessary all-nighters and littering the West Wing with empty pizza boxes and cans of Diet Coke. And it was true that the atmosphere was, well, rather loose. Clinton's daily schedule was . . . fluid, to say the least. Meetings were interminable, often inconclusive, and open to almost anyone on staff who happened to walk in. There was, one weekend in the spring, a seven-hour meeting on Bosnia that resulted in no significant policy action; there were similar seminars on health care and a variety of other topics, as well as the constant, ever-shifting anxieties of the budget fight. Bentsen called Clinton "the meetingest fellow I've ever met."

He was also the most dilatory: The President was almost never on time, and quite often more than an hour behind schedule. He seemed perpetually caught up in the moment—talking, listening, empathizing—unable to distinguish between large problems and trivial ones, unable to set his priorities or make decisions; the question of whether Richard Holbrooke or former

Vice President Walter Mondale should be Ambassador to Japan was debated on three separate occasions in the Oval Office before it was finally resolved (Mondale went to Japan; Holbrooke, Germany). One day, William Galston—a Progressive Policy Institute thinker who had joined the White House staff as a domestic policy advisor—actually walked out of one of his rare meetings with the President, which had been delayed for two hours, after passing a note to McLarty: "I promised my son I'd go to his Little League game."

Senators John McCain and Bob Kerrey would never forget their first visit to the Clinton White House to discuss normalization of relations with Vietnam. They had to wait forty-five minutes for the meeting to begin and then Clinton, who seemed intensely interested in their memories of combat and their feelings about the war, was distracted by young aides who moved in and out, passing notes, whispering in the President's ear and worse, chatting among themselves. Kerrey later told me he wanted to grab George Stephanopoulos by the lapels and say, "Listen, kid, you're in the presence of the President of the United States. Show some respect!"

Stephanopoulos, the public face of the Administration's perceived callowness, was thirty years old when he joined the campaign staff in 1991, one of Clinton's first hires. Previously, he had worked for then House Majority Leader Richard Gephardt—and he reflected Gephardt's liberal, Midwestern populism. Stephanopoulos was the most likely object of the President's volcanic, if fleeting, rages, but he was also extremely powerful during the first few years: the spiritual leader of the hardest workers in the White House—the pizza and Diet Coke brigade—who *were* younger, more accessible to the press (especially to Bob Woodward and the late Anne Devroy of the *Washington Post*) and more liberal than the members of the economic team; more liberal, in most cases, than the President himself. Stephanopoulos was a committed pessimist and a fierce partisan, convinced that any attempt to cooperate with the Republicans in Congress was not only craven, but also foolhardy—a position that seemed justified that first year as the Republicans proved every bit as intransigent as George had told Clinton they would be. Over time, Stephanopoulos's tactical sense of the Congress would prove his greatest strength but also his greatest weakness, since it was accompanied by a constricted, legislative sense of the power of the presidency. He seemed to stare down Pennsylvania Avenue through the wrong end of the telescope—overestimating the importance of legislation as a marker of success, underestimating the President's power to transform the public square into his own personal theater, unaware that the very definition of victory or defeat could be shaped by the White House.

But then, Clinton himself didn't quite understand the true potential of the office yet, either. By late spring of 1993, with the budget battle far more difficult than he had anticipated and with the press intent on rehearsing an endless stream of "White House in Chaos" stories, the President decided he was in desperate need of some experienced help. He suddenly reshuffled the White House staff, adding David Gergen—a Republican who had served in the Ford and Reagan administrations—to the "message" operation. At the same time, he decided to move Stephanopoulos out of public view and he made Dee Dee Myers the day-to-day press secretary. "The President told me that he was distressed by the fact that he was out of position," Gergen recalled. "He thought he was perceived as being too far left."

Gergen, in fact, was profoundly postpartisan, more a member of The Third Way New Whatever party than an adherent to either of the traditional philosophies—but his arrival was seen as fresh evidence (particularly among liberals) that Clinton didn't really believe in anything. And while Stephanopoulos himself was happy to be relieved of the daily press feeding frenzy, the Stephanopoulite faction of the staff was enraged by Gergen's arrival and saw the newcomer as an alien implant to be rejected as quickly as possible—which he was: Gergen lasted less than a year in the White House.

"I found Clinton's style of leadership very distressing at first," Gergen later told me. "The Republican presidents I'd served had a clear vision of where they were going, and their staffs reflected that. But Clinton had all sorts of people at the table, all sorts of opinions. He had to hear from 'New' Democrats and 'Old' Democrats and feminists and the union folks—and it offended my old-school style. But I eventually realized that this was a new, postmodern style of leadership, and that it was probably a good thing. In fact, I believe it was a reflection of the country's diversity: It's possible that all future presidents will make their decisions this way."

Which was one way to look at it. A rather generous way. In truth, Clinton's management style wasn't nearly so intentional as Gergen made it sound. It was a consequence of two character traits that his aides found distressing: his inability to deliver bad news and his inability to make up his mind. A murky, Machiavellian atmosphere prevailed in the White House as a result. Messages were delivered obliquely, there were factions and fragments of factions, circles within circles and constant conspiracies, often involving the First Lady, whose influence was overwhelming but rarely open. "A chipper President would arrive at the office in the morning," Gergen wrote in his memoir of presidential service. "A phone would ring. It was a call from upstairs at the residence. He would listen, utter a few words, but as we started back to work, his mood would darken, his attention would wander and hot words would spew out. Had we seen the outrageous things his enemies were saying about him now? Why hadn't we attacked? Why was he working so hard and getting so little credit? Why was his staff screwing him again? *What*, I would wonder, had she said to him now?"

CHAPTER
THREE

In the summer of 1993, I received word from several of Al Gore's staff members that the Vice President had something to show me. It turned out to be an ashtray. More precisely, it was a standard, regulation, federal government "ash receiver, tobacco, desk type," and Gore had ten pages of regulations to prove it.

"Can you believe this?" he said, flipping through the regulations as we sat in his West Wing office, a huge photo of the Earth on the wall. "It's incredible. This is what you have to do if you want to sell the government an ashtray. . . . Now, here's my favorite. This is the specification for how you test it." You put the ashtray on a plank, he said, "a maple plank. It has to be maple, 44.5 millimeters thick." And you hit it with a steel punch "point ground to a sixty percent included angle" and a hammer. "The specimen should break into a small number of irregularly shaped pieces, no greater than thirty-five." Gore was losing it now, belly-laughing. "But wait! Now we get to the specification of the pieces!" To be counted as regulation shards, they must be "6.4 millimeters or more, on any three of its adjacent edges . . ."

Several weeks later, Gore actually shattered a government ashtray on *Late Night with David Letterman*—one of his more felicitous appearances in a painfully awkward public career. The Vice President received rave reviews for his dry, self-deprecating wit, but there was a serious political purpose behind the vaudeville: Gore was not only promoting his "Reinventing Government" reform portfolio (which unfortunately came to be known as REGO), but he was also in the midst of a fierce, three-way competition to set the President's priorities for the fall—a competition he seemed destined to lose, since the other two contenders were the First Lady, who wanted her husband to focus (like a laser beam) on selling her health insurance reform program; and the economic team, which knew that the effort to round up votes for NAFTA would require some very labor-intensive lobbying by the President.

Gore agreed that NAFTA had to be the top priority, so the real battle was against the First Lady—Reinventing Government vs. Health Care, New Democrats vs. Old. Indeed, Gore had quietly emerged as the most important New Democrat in the Administration: He had sided with the "deficit hawks" on the budget and was the most eloquent advocate for an aggressive American military presence in the Balkans. He was an ambitious and intelligent politician, if not a particularly gifted one. He had helped save the Clinton candidacy in 1992—his selection as Vice President was seen as a gust of fresh air, creating the first all–Baby Boom presidential ticket, reinforcing the sense of newness and moderation, and the Southernness of the Clinton project. Indeed, there were those who believed that the ticket should have been reversed, with Gore the presidential nominee.

But they were wrong: Gore had a genius for subservience (and also, unfortunately, the submerged, constricted anger that often accompanies such passivity). He was a shy, uncomfortable man, who once admitted to me that he probably wouldn't have become a politician if his father—who had been an esteemed, if gaseous, liberal senator from Tennessee—hadn't been in the business. Even as Vice President, Gore seemed all tangled up in his sonhood; he admitted being fascinated by a book called *The Drama of the Gifted Child* by Alice Miller. He seemed the eternal protégé, more a son than a father figure, more a student—the world's best student—than a teacher. He was a natural number two.

The Reinventing Government project was perfect for him, very worthy if eminently vice presidential: Presidents usually have more important things to worry about than how the government actually works. But Reinventing Government was a particular favorite of New Democrats, who loved the idea of a direct assault upon the ancient paradigm of federal bureaucracy. It also seemed good politics. Horror stories about endless red tape and other governmental abominations were popular with the public and easy to sell on the evening news. If the Clinton administration could convince America that it was serious about attacking the mythic federal troika—waste, fraud, and abuse—it might be able to build the credibility to propose new "investments" like universal health insurance.

Gore, who had a passion for bloodless, technical issues, pursued this one with great energy and determination; he was a font of Stupid Government Stories. In the process, his staff became a haven for Progressive Policy Institute wonks: Elaine Kamarck was in charge of Reinventing Government and David Osborne—who had written the book that popularized the phrase—was brought along to write the report detailing the Clinton administration's plans to make government more "entrepreneurial." Indeed, the project eventually would have a significant, if underappreciated, impact on federal governance. The federal workforce would be reduced by about 350,000 and an estimated $157 billion saved. Equally important, 16,000 pages of bureaucratic regulations would be tossed—including some of the more famous governmental snafus, like the purchasing regulations at the Pentagon that resulted in $700 toilet seats and $150 hammers. Gore was hoping to announce all this during a weeklong promotion featuring the President just after Labor Day—but there was strong opposition from the Hillary camp and Stephanopoulites, who saw REGO as (1) a diversion of the President's time away from health care and (2) demagogic, and ultimately ineffective, government bashing.

There was a sandbox intensity to the internal struggle. New Democrats were particularly embittered, even though Clinton had taken the DLC line on deficit reduction and was about to do the same on free trade. But the Clinton inner circle seemed dominated by anachronistic liberals—the young Stephanopoulites and the Hillary cadre. The First Lady's extremely powerful, if dimly perceived, presence was especially frustrating to the New Dems, who hoped the President would take up welfare reform before he dove into health care (the theory here was similar to the Reinventing Government argument: If Clinton could clean up the welfare system, which was widely perceived by the "forgotten middle class" as a government subsidy for the indolent and the irresponsible, he might be able to build a constituency for new forms of government activism). But, given the First Lady's involvement, there was no chance that the health care crusade would be postponed.

Gore did win a small victory, launching REGO on the White House lawn with Clinton in early September; the backdrop was two forklifts piled high with stacks of government regulations. The event was quickly forgotten, though. And the rivalry between the Vice President and the First Lady—and even the campaign to pass NAFTA—were soon put into perspective by a completely unexpected series of foreign policy crises and embarrassments.

A new, complicated and occasionally combustible post–Cold War world was looming, and Clinton had spent too little time schooling himself in the vagaries of foreign policy during his first nine months in office. His lack of preparation, he later admitted, would have dire consequences—he would blame himself for the only lives lost in battle during his entire presidency.

BILL CLINTON WAS NEVER AS inept or uninterested in diplomatic matters as his critics charged. But his interest was intermittent, in part because the world he faced wasn't as immediately threatening as it once had been. There was no longer the danger of a nuclear confrontation with the Russians. The thorniest foreign policy issues were, almost by definition, peripheral. They revolved around the question of intervention: How actively should the United States involve itself in local disputes—often internecine, ethnic disputes—in remote parts of the world? Some, like Clinton's National Security Advisor Anthony Lake, argued that the internal weakness of potential rivals like Russia and China, and the possibility of anarchy in historically crucial regions like the Balkans, were now the greatest threats to American interests abroad. But nettlesome, eternal problems like the civil war in Bosnia or the military repression in Haiti seemed less immediate than the daily struggle to pass a budget (or the internal bickering over Mrs. Clinton's health plan). The selection of a flaccid, almost purposefully obscure foreign policy team seemed further evidence of Clinton's relative lack of interest in the area.

Both Lake and Warren Christopher, the Secretary of State, were intelligent and experienced diplomats; Secretary of Defense Les Aspin had been the most creative military reformer and strategist in Congress. But all three were uncomfortable in public and it was hard to know if their discomfort was congenital or the consequence of serving an uncertain, uninterested President. Lake found television news programs so banal and superficial that he generally refused to appear on them; Christopher would appear, but he seemed comatose; Aspen also appeared, but he was twitchy and unkempt. In private, the situation wasn't much different: All three men were curiously averse to recommending decisive presidential action, especially in military affairs (to the dismay of Al Gore, in particular; and Gore eventually replaced Christopher as the Administration's primary foreign policy voice on the Sunday morning talk shows). By contrast, General Colin

Powell, then completing his term as chairman of the Joint Chiefs of Staff, had no trouble expressing himself or promoting his views, and his views—on gays in the military, and Bosnia, and Somalia—tended to be dominant.

Powell's reluctance to use military force was well known. But his advice to the President on the situation in Somalia was a strange exception. The operation had begun during the Bush administration as a humanitarian intervention to alleviate a famine, but the multinational peacekeepers, operating under the aegis of the United Nations, soon found themselves acting as a severely constrained police force, trying to maintain order in the midst of local political chaos. This gradual, unplanned evolution gave the world a fabulous new military expression: "mission creep."

Remarkably, it was Colin Powell who allowed this particular mission to creep. "It was a warrior response," said a Pentagon official who attended the meetings where the decisions were made. "In early June, twenty-four Pakistani were killed by the Somalis and Powell just flipped his position. He began arguing for the inserting of more units, and ultimately Delta Force."

This proved to be one of Colin Powell's less distinguished moments. His term as chairman of the Joint Chiefs of Staff ended while the mission was still in progress. He might have delayed his departure to see the mission to its end; Bill Clinton certainly wanted him to stay. But Powell departed on September 30, and three days later there was a botched Delta Force commando operation in which eighteen Americans were killed. The Clinton administration, under intense pressure from Congress, abandoned Somalia.

It seems clear that Bill Clinton was daunted by Colin Powell. He never questioned Powell's strategy or tactics in Somalia. He almost seemed unaware of the details of the mission. Indeed, this was the first real indication of Clinton's discomfort about military matters—a result, perhaps, of his avoidance of the draft as a young man (even his inability to salute with crisp, martial precision became a public issue). On Somalia, Clinton told me in July 2000, when he was still President, that he agreed to Powell's final escalation, the use of Delta Force guerrillas in the hunt for the Somali warlord Mohammed Farah Aidid. "There was an operational decision made there which, if I had to do it again, I might do what we did then, but I'd do it in a different way," the President said. "General Powell came in and said you ought to do this—and then he retired. He left the next week. And I'm not blaming him, I'm just saying he was gone. So what happened was we had this huge battle in broad daylight where hundreds of Somalis were killed and we lost eighteen soldiers in what was a UN action. I think I'll always regret . . . I don't know if I could have saved those lives or not, but I would have handled it in a different way if I'd had more experience. I know I would have. If we were going to do that now, I'd say I need to know what's involved here, and let's do this the way we planned out the military action we took against Saddam Hussein, for example, or the military actions I took to try to get Osama bin Laden's training camps."

The last part of Clinton's statement—about Iraqi president Saddam Hussein and the terrorist Osama bin Laden—seemed unconvincing at the time, and it seems downright embarrassing after the terrorist attacks on New York and Washington, D.C., on September 11, 2001. Both the Iraq and bin Laden campaigns involved the long-distance use of air power and no risk to American lives. Neither was, ultimately, successful. Indeed, the military and intelligence communities were convinced that the missions were worse than futile: They only served to strengthen the reputations of Saddam Hussein and Osama bin Laden in the Arab world. "To personalize a conflict with an Arab leader is to enhance his stature," said Dr. Jerrold Post, a specialist in the psychology of terrorism who has profiled both Saddam Hussein and bin Laden. "Every time we struck and failed to defeat [them], [they] could say [they] had beaten the United States once again."

But neither the public nor the military seemed willing to risk American lives in pursuit of threats that were both abstract and unthinkable. It is easy to say, in retrospect, that Clinton should have foreseen the danger and *led* the nation in a more aggressive, riskier war against international terrorism. He certainly could have been more sure-handed; he surely could have done more. But it is difficult to locate another American President who was able to rouse a happy, peaceful populace to sacrifice their lives in the service of an abstraction (John Kennedy, Lyndon Johnson, and Richard Nixon tried to counter a mirage of "communism" in Vietnam, and their efforts ripped the nation apart in ways that haven't quite healed thirty years later). The American way of war seems—unfortunately, or maybe not—to be a full-blooded, lethal response only after the country has been taken by surprise.

THE BATTLE IN SOMALIA OCCURRED on October 3, 1993. Within a week, there was another blunder, this time in Haiti. An American ship, the *USS Harlan County*, was about to arrive in Port-au-Prince, carrying lightly armed forces whose purpose, agreed upon in advance by the Haitian junta, was to "train" a new civilian police force. But an unofficial and potentially lethal welcoming committee—pistol-carrying emissaries of the junta—appeared on the dock to prevent the arrival. The loss of more American lives in a dubious cause seemed imminent; the ship was ordered not to dock. And then, after several days of dithering just outside the harbor, the *Harlan County* turned around and came home. "A total fuckup," Lake would recall. "We were double-crossed by General [Raoul] Cedras," the leader of the junta. "But it was our fault: We had sent the ship out with zero military support."

Both Lake and Christopher immediately offered to resign after these calamities, which was good internal politics; Aspin, less prompt with his tender, was the one who was asked to leave. He was succeeded by his deputy, William Perry, who was better organized and more competent, but every bit as colorless as the others—and the Administration's uncertainty overseas, especially in the Balkans, continued to be an embarrassment. It wasn't until 1995, when the United Nations peacekeeping mission appeared to be collapsing in Bosnia (and Clinton found out that the United States was committed to the extremely expensive, potentially dangerous, and politically disastrous mission of extracting the peacekeepers—and, thereby, presiding over a historic international defeat at the hands of ethnic thugs) that the President was convinced to take action. He launched an aerial assault against the Bosnian Serbs, who capitulated soon after cruise missiles were fired into the city Banja Luka—the Serbs were astonished and terrified by the ability of the missiles to navigate the local street grid and pick out specific targets. Clinton also launched Richard Holbrooke into the region, a diplomat whose aggressive, and ultimately successful, pursuit of a Bosnian peace stood in stark contrast to the Lake–Christopher diffidence. Shuttling daily from Belgrade to Zagreb to Sarajevo, Holbrooke negotiated a cease-fire in the autumn of 1995. That winter, at a United States Air Force base in Dayton, Ohio, he coaxed a more permanent power-sharing agreement from the Serbs, Croats, and Bosnian Muslims. It was the first, most intricate, and, arguably, the most significant foreign policy success of the Clinton administration.

Over time, the President's handling of foreign policy would become less wobbly (although his handling of national security issues remained sketchy and uncertain). He came to know the other world leaders as fellow politicians; he had a particular affection for outsized fellows like Boris Yeltsin and Helmut Kohl. He enjoyed hashing over common domestic dilemmas with them—as more of his peers began to describe themselves as Third Way leaders, their opponents took on a similar cast as well: trade union conservatives on the left and religious extremists on the right. Before long, Clinton was preeminent in gatherings of world leaders; an older brother to Britain's Tony Blair and an unofficial advisor to countless others. James Carville, who found there was an international market for his services, was perpetually amazed by the power of Clinton's name: "Every country I went to," he recalled, "the first thing the candidate wanted to do was make it public that he'd hired me. It was the

Clinton association. They wanted people to know that they were close to Bill Clinton. It was a political plus all over the world."

The members of Clinton's second-term foreign policy team—Secretary of State Madeleine Albright; National Security Advisor Samuel Berger, and the Republican, William Cohen, as Secretary of Defense—were, arguably, less talented than their predecessors but also less restrained: Under their watch, the President became far more willing to use force, particularly the remote control violence wrought by the cruise missile. This new aggressiveness masked a continuing dispute with the military, which seemed unwilling to do anything but launch missiles from great distances or bombs from high altitudes. "After Somalia, the military leaders were extremely frightened," said General Wesley Clark, who led the NATO bombing campaign in Kosovo. "The attitude was 'If you take losses, you're a loser. Your career is over.' It was assumed that politicians wouldn't support you, that they'd run away as soon as there were body bags. That became an article of faith."

The Clinton national security team, especially Albright and Berger, were continually frustrated by this. "When it came to closework," one Clinton official said, referring to military operations that required a high degree of precision and risk, "the culture and mind-set of the military was 'That's what the CIA is for.' When we asked the Pentagon to capture Radovan Karadzic, the Bosnian Serb leader who had been charged as a war criminal by the Hague tribunal, they wouldn't go near it. When we asked them to do special ops on terrorists operating in a semiurban environment, their response was 'That's not what we do. We're not organized for that. We need a brigade.' "

Of course, the President could have *ordered* them to do any of these things.

Clinton did seem much more comfortable when it came to negotiating, if never quite resolving, disputes in the Middle East, Africa, and Northern Ireland. His policies toward Russia and China reflected a broad, bipartisan consensus—encouragement of democracy in Russia (while also expanding the North Atlantic Treaty Organization into the former Soviet satellites of Poland, Hungary, and the Czech Republic); and free trade with China, in the hope that an expanding free market would create a more assertive Chinese middle class.

Eventually, Clinton would visit more countries than any previous American President, but he remained too much of a politician—impatient, imprecise, not careful enough about the details—to be entirely successful as a diplomat. The most striking foreign policy image of the Clinton presidency, the reluctant handshake between Yitzhak Rabin and Yasser Arafat on the White House lawn (with the President between them, shepherding them closer, arms outstretched), was illusory: The real negotiations had taken place earlier, in Norway, without American involvement.

"There weren't any major disasters," said Senator John McCain, summarizing the most common criticism of Clinton's foreign policy at the end of his eight years in office. "But you wonder if the seeds of future problems have been sown. He butterflies from issue to issue, and foreign policy just doesn't work that way. It has to be steady, concentrated, precise. He goes to Beijing and calls the Chinese our 'strategic partners.' Well, you wonder what the Japanese, who *are* our strategic partners, think about that. He 'wins ugly' in Kosovo by bombing from fifteen thousand feet, a policy I considered immoral, and then the Russians feel free to use the same policy in Chechnya."

McCain's point was prescient but incomplete. The difficult decisions, especially those that involved the use of force, did seem either rushed or belated—poorly planned and, in the case of Iraq and bin Laden, dangerously inconclusive. Other Republicans, less sophisticated and more ideological than McCain, also criticized Clinton for his willingness to engage in multilateral treaty-making. They argued that the United States had reached an unprecedented pinnacle of power and didn't really need to negotiate its positions on issues ranging from global warming to a missile defense shield with other countries, especially if that meant making serious concessions. This seemed a crude, and rather improbable, doctrine even before it was adopted by Clinton's successor, George W. Bush; in practice, it proved gratuitously arrogant and potentially dangerous. In his first months in office, Bush—or, perhaps, his foreign policy advisors—publicly trashed the Kyoto treaty on global warming, the Anti-Ballistic Missile treaty, and an array of other agreements (all the way down to a United Nations protocol on the sale of small arms to developing countries). The "unilateralists" argued that these were flawed, sometimes foolish, treaties, and that was undoubtedly true—Clinton had no intention of implementing Kyoto as it was written and he was testing, however cautiously, a missile-defense shield, but he also understood the long-term value of diplomatic humility, of not making unnecessary enemies, of pursuing American interests within the context of multilateral organizations (and he knew that if these often fatuous processes were respected, American interests would almost always carry the day). There was a puerile, unnecessarily confrontational quality to Bush's early foreign policy that made Republican complaints about Clinton's diplomatic "ineptitude" seem ridiculous in retrospect. And Bush's policy quickly changed—it became more multilateral, more Clintonian—after the terror attacks on September 2001.

Even the most intemperate Republicans had to acknowledge, however, that Clinton did leave one permanent, if underappreciated, mark on American foreign policy: He rearranged the traditional priorities, raising economic issues to the same level of importance as strategic affairs.

THERE IS A SUBTLE DIFFERENCE between "internationalism," which refers to the relationships between nations, and "globalism," which is a more fluid, Information Age concept that presupposes the primacy of economic affairs—and Clinton was, arguably, the first "globalist" President. Certainly, he was far more confident when it came to the use of American economic power overseas—to preserve economic stability in Latin America and Asia, for example—than he was about the projection of American diplomatic or military force. "There were two things that struck me when I first met Clinton in 1991," Anthony Lake recalled. "The first had to do with a foreign policy speech he was preparing to deliver at Georgetown University. I had written some language for it and he would say 'I agree with that' if he liked something as opposed to 'that's good.' The other thing was more unsettling. He kept saying, 'Foreign policy is domestic policy.' That was not an immediately attractive concept for someone like me, and it took me more than a year to understand all the implications of it—but he was right."

Indeed, foreign policy had traditionally been practiced by a secular priesthood of academics, diplomats, and financiers who saw their work as different, higher, and certainly more important than the tawdry business of domestic policy (which was considered a lowly *legislative* activity, as opposed to the distinctly *executive* nature of foreign affairs). This was, of course, nonsense—especially in a world where global economic trends had an increasing impact on America's domestic economy and where America's "soft" power (that is, its cultural and economic power) had become a more pervasive influence than its military force.

Clinton assumed that economic globalization was inevitable. He also believed in the classical theory of free trade: Lower tariffs would result in lower prices, greater exports, and a stronger economy. "It's so wonderful when an economic theory turns out to be right," Lawrence Summers, who succeeded Robert Rubin as Treasury Secretary, would later crow. "The economic benefits of the tariff reductions we negotiated during the Clinton administration represents the largest tax cut in the history of the world."

Summers was a Harvard economist; he paid no political price for his faith in the theory (nor, for that matter, did most House Republicans, whose constituencies were not concerned with the issue; South Carolina Republicans like Strom Thurmond are protectionist because of the prominence of the textile industry there).

The President faced a more difficult political reality. The benefits of free trade weren't so obvious to unionized workers in mature industries like steel and automobiles, particularly in the Midwest. The deficits of free trade were far more apparent, especially as whole factories closed and relocated in Mexico and Asia. As a result, most Democrats—especially the liberal populists in the House—were vehemently opposed to any lowering of tariffs (as were the Stephanopoulites in the White House). And, in the autumn of 1993, they had a powerful ally in the First Lady—who didn't really oppose the North American Free Trade Agreement but was afraid that her health insurance proposal would falter if it wasn't promoted exclusively. Clinton, inimitably, wanted to do both; but the trade agreement with Mexico, which had to be passed immediately or expire, took precedence.

In September 1993, the President made a series of striking public appearances. There was the Rabin–Arafat handshake on the White House lawn and then, a day later, Clinton stood with three former presidents—Ford, Carter, and Bush—at a White House ceremony in support of NAFTA. His discussion of the issues at stake was so lucid that George Bush (the Elder), who followed him to the podium, was moved to say, "Now I know why he's inside looking out and I'm outside looking in."

Clinton's presentation of the health insurance plan to a joint session of Congress eight days later, on September 22, was equally impressive. Early polls showed that a majority of the public supported universal coverage, but the politics remained difficult, at best. Shortly after the speech, Clinton was visited by Lane Kirkland, the president of the AFL-CIO, who said, "Mr. President, that was a terrific speech, and we have $10 million we'd like to spend on television ads promoting your health care plan. . . . Of course, if you insist on going ahead with NAFTA, we're going to take the $10 million and spend it in opposition to that."

Clinton refused to budge. He spent much of the autumn working to pass NAFTA, but there was a significant price to success: Once again, he had used a significant amount of political capital by asking for a difficult vote from the Democrats in Congress (indeed, it is quite likely that his Republican predecessor, George Bush, who negotiated the treaty, would never have been able to get it ratified by the Democratic Congress). And there was a more cosmic, long-term cost to his difficult, first-year victories: "We didn't know enough about how the system worked," Clinton would later concede. "It can only digest so much at once. We did the big economic plan and NAFTA in ninety-three. But trying to push through health care at that point was a mistake. . . . I should have done welfare reform before we tried health care. If we had done welfare reform and the crime bill in ninety-four, the Democrats might have had something to run on in the fall. . . . But I think in the beginning, for the first two years, I was pushing a lot of rocks up the hill. I was obsessed . . . I was trying to get as much done as quickly as I could and also trying to learn on the job, learn how to get the White House functioning."

And yet, for just a moment at the end of 1993, Clinton seemed to be succeeding on all fronts. His approval ratings, which had dived in the spring, rose in the fall. He made a stunning, impromptu performance before a group of black ministers in Memphis—perhaps the best speech an American President

has ever delivered to a black audience, and also one of the toughest. He spoke informally, but without patronizing; and he spoke
brazenly, presuming to know what Martin Luther King might
say if he were still alive: " 'I fought for freedom,' he would say,
'but not for the freedom of people to kill each other with reckless abandon, not for the freedom of children to have children,
and the fathers of the children to walk away and abandon them
as if they don't amount to anything. . . . That is not what I lived
and died for.' "

The reception was sensational; the ministers seemed to sense,
as many African-Americans did, that the President of the United
States was *family*. He was willing to confront black audiences
with some difficult truths—about the need for welfare reform
(which was always a big applause line when he spoke to socially
conservative black middle-class audiences) and parental responsibility—but he was equally insistent on the need for racial tolerance and a determined government effort to promote diversity.
He was passionate, and passionately optimistic, about the ad-
vantages of a multiracial society in a global economy: "Our diversity is a strength, not a weakness," he would say. This seemed
fanciful in 1993, a time when many sophisticated observers were
afraid that the homogeneous Japanese and Germans represented
the economic future (indeed, Clinton had to endure a lecture
from the Japanese Prime Minister about the need for fiscal discipline at his first international economic summit, the G-7 meeting in 1993).

Over time, though, the Japanese and Germans faltered, and
the creativity and optimism of a new generation of immigrants
transformed America's traditional, binary racial dilemma—black

and white, separate and unequal—into a fabulous polychrome. Toward the end of Clinton's time in office, the President made a tour of impoverished areas, hoping to encourage businesses to create "New Markets" in poor communities. The Reverend Jesse Jackson traveled with the President and, one day in the Mississippi Delta, Jackson and I watched a blithely multiracial crowd await the President's speech.

"Look at that!" Jackson said, nudging me in the ribs. "Isn't it glorious!"

"What do you mean?" I asked. "You've seen multiracial crowds down here before."

"Yes, but now they're *talking* to each other," Jackson said, and then he whispered, "And you know what else, they're *sleeping* with each other, too."

Clinton did not create this new atmosphere. Indeed, his formal efforts to "do" something about race—his second-term "commission" to study the problem, for example—tended to slide into irrelevance. But his acceptance—and more than that, his *appreciation* of African-Americans—created the subtext for a new American tolerance, especially among young people, who really did seem to understand, as the twentieth century ended, that the nation's racial diversity was not only a significant advantage in the global marketplace but also a source of social and cultural creativity at home.

THE MEMPHIS SPEECH WAS THE emotional apogee of Clinton's first year in office, but there had been another, equally telling, moment in an earlier Clinton speech. In

September, when the President had presented his health plan to a joint session of Congress, the wrong speech—his State of the Union message from six months earlier—was in the TelePrompTer. He had to stand in front of Congress, and the nation, and *make it up* until the correct speech was found. The consultant Paul Begala would later ask him, "What were you thinking when that happened?"

"I was thinking, 'Lord, you're really testing me.'" Clinton smiled and slowly shook his head, relishing the near-death experience. "Ohhh-kayyyy!"

CHAPTER

FOUR

Bill Clinton has a favorite joke. He told it on the campaign trail in both his presidential campaigns and, at the end of his presidency, he told it again to me: "A guy is walking along the edge of the Grand Canyon and he falls off. He's hurtling down hundreds of feet to certain death and he looks up and grabs this twig, and it breaks his fall. He heaves a sigh of relief . . . and then, all of a sudden, he sees the roots coming loose. He looks up to the sky and says, 'God, why me? I'm a good person. I've taken care of my family. I've paid all my taxes. I've worked all my life. Why me?' And this thunderous voice says, 'Son, there's just something about you that I don't like.'"

We had been talking about the pyrotechnic hatred that Clinton inspired among his opponents. I asked the President if he had been surprised by the poisonous atmosphere in Washington. "I know things now that I didn't know then," he began, but then he had another thought. "Actually, I did know something. In

1990, before I decided to run, I got a call from a guy in the Bush White House who told me not to run. Bush was at like eighty percent in the polls, and I was saying how the President should use his popularity to fix the economy. And, after about five minutes, this guy says, 'Now let's just cut the crap. We've looked at this crowd'—all the Democrats considering a run against Bush in 1992—'and we can beat them all. You're the only one who might cause us some trouble and so, if you do run, we're going to have to knock you out early.'

"After I got here and started dealing with them, I realized that the Republicans had been in power since Nixon—with the exception of Jimmy Carter, whose election they saw purely as a function of Watergate." Clinton paused to praise the Carter presidency as a spiritual precursor of the New Democratic movement, and then he returned to the subject at hand. "They figured there'd never be another Democratic President. I really think a lot of them thought they could hold the White House until a third party came along to basically offer a competing vision. So they just never saw me as a legitimate person."

From the beginning of his presidency, there was indeed the sense—radiating from the Gingrich wing of the Republican Party, and also from a group of rabid, unflagging Clinton-haters in Arkansas—that the new President was a usurper who had managed to hoodwink the American public. He was to be opposed at every turn, by any means necessary, and, if possible, destroyed. "It's true," Senator Bob Dole, perhaps the most respected Republican politician of the Clinton era, later confirmed. "We had a pretty hard-right group in the party who were just never going to accept him."

Actually, the utterly noxious atmosphere that greeted Clinton when he arrived in Washington had been gathering for some time—for at least two decades, in fact, ever since the Watergate scandal. American politics had turned rancid with hearings and special prosecutors, accusations, and diatribes directed against public figures. The accusations and diatribes were nothing new, of course; they were as old as the republic. But now they were accompanied by endless legal procedures. "There have always been political scandals," observed Gordon Wood of Brown University, the preeminent historian of the American revolutionary period. "There have been periods of severe partisanship and vitriolic rhetoric. But I don't think we've ever had a time in American history like this one, with so many prominent figures facing legal action, and with politics criminalized."

By the time Bill Clinton arrived in Washington, scandals—sometimes over the most niggling misdemeanors—had become the defining events of public life, often more compelling and significant than elections. A fierce, undeclared war raged between Democrats and Republicans over what was loosely called "ethics," but which usually involved something less than outright illegality—"the appearance of impropriety" was the standard media shorthand. The assault on Clinton was the inevitable climax of an irrational fever—the governmental equivalent of the Salem witch trials—that had engulfed the political community, a form of madness choreographed by the most extreme elements in both parties and cheered on by a happily voracious press. In the process, two Speakers of the House, Jim Wright and Newt Gingrich, were driven from office. Three Republican Supreme Court nominees—Douglas Ginsburg, Robert Bork, and Clarence

Thomas—were subjected to severe ideological and personal assaults. Five members of Clinton's Cabinet were pursued by special prosecutors. A slew of Cabinet-level nominees were shot down for reasons trivial or incomprehensible (and, in any case, soon forgotten). And, just below the level of media attention, hundreds of other government officials were investigated on charges—often frivolous complaints, filed anonymously—that were brought to the attention of the Inspectors General in the various cabinet departments. Indeed, partisan legal harassment had become a major industry in Washington, providing crude entertainment and satisfying careers for thousands of shortsighted practitioners.

All this in a nation's capital that was, by most accounts, far less corrupt than it had ever been. "Compare this Congress to the one in 1950, during the era that most of the old-timers consider the Golden Age of civil discourse," Senator Joseph Biden, a Democrat from Delaware, said. "Those guys were taking handouts, honoraria, junkets. When I came here in 1973, Jacob Javits—a distinguished senator—was making money from a private law practice. You don't think he'd be under investigation today? By comparison, these new guys are squeaky clean. I can't stand most of the SOBs—they're ideologues, they practice Khmer Rouge politics—but they are the cleanest bunch of politicians this capital has ever seen."

The Clinton era is likely to be remembered more for the ferocity of its prosecutions than for the severity of its crimes—and if there was one politician who personified that ferocity more than any other, it was Newt Gingrich of Georgia. His story and the demolition of public civility that deformed the Clinton era are inextricably entwined.

LATE IN THE AFTERNOON of May 15, 1984, Speaker of the House Thomas P. (Tip) O'Neill, a politician known for his even-tempered charm, publicly and unexpectedly blew his stack. The moment was astonishing for several reasons. Speakers of the House rarely speak. They almost never set aside the gavel and step down to take the microphone in the well; when they do, it usually is to provide a dignified conclusion to a debate of national import. But this was a spontaneous moment of rage. O'Neill rumbled down the center aisle of the chamber, seized the lectern and began to excoriate a fellow representative—an obscure back-bencher, at that—for what he believed to be a severe breach of decorum. His face lobster-red and his finger wagging, O'Neill began to yell, over the derisive hoots of the Republican opposition, at a junior member from Georgia. It should come as no surprise that the member in question was none other than Newt Gingrich.

"It was Newt's first big victory," said Vin Weber, a Gingrich ally who was a young congressman from Minnesota at the time. "And it was a huge mistake on Tip's part." O'Neill had, in fact, been frustrated by three developments that were to become prominent features of the late-twentieth-century political landscape: a new generation of disrespectful Baby Boom politicians from the suburbs (O'Neill was a titanic urban anachronism from the Boston area); a more partisan and ideological Republican party, with a rising crop of Southerners to lead it; and the arrival within the Congress of a disruptive new medium—television.

In point of fact, O'Neill had gone berserk over the Republicans' use of C-SPAN. A week earlier Gingrich had made a late-night speech in which he seemed to question the patriotism of several Democrats, by name. The chamber was almost empty, but his real audience was cable television viewers across the country. With the camera fixed, by House rules, on the orator, Gingrich was able to challenge the Democrats to defend their votes against defense spending. There was no way for the audience to know that the Democrats in question didn't respond because they weren't there. O'Neill decided to change the C-SPAN rules without consulting the Republicans: He would allow cameras to pan the empty chamber. Gingrich rose to protest the "unilateral" decision, which led to O'Neill's angry response. "You deliberately stood in the well of this House and took on these members when you knew they weren't here," the Speaker shouted. "It's un-American! It's the lowest thing I've heard in my thirty-two years here!"

Chaos ensued. Representative Trent Lott of Mississippi, a Republican who later became the Senate Majority Leader, demanded that O'Neill's comments be "taken down" since they violated House rules prohibiting derogatory remarks about fellow members, and Representative Joseph Moakley of Massachusetts, an O'Neill protégé who had taken the chair, reluctantly agreed. The Republicans, downtrodden after thirty years in the minority, were stunned and delighted: One of their most outspoken and least popular members had humiliated the Speaker of the House. Gingrich was given a standing ovation as he returned to his seat.

"That was the opening shot in the war," Weber later recalled. "The Democrats were arrogant to the point of corruption, and Newt's idea was to expose the arrogance and corruption for what it was. It was guerrilla war, and I don't think we could have won the House in 1994 without those sorts of tactics. But the victory came at a price, and the price was a loss of civility."

THE BEGINNING OF THE ERA of Bad Feelings is usually associated with Watergate, but its roots probably can be traced back a decade earlier. "The trouble began when we political scientists finally got our wish—'responsible' political parties instead of broad, nonideological coalitions," said Nelson Polsby, a political scientist at the University of California at Berkeley. "The idea was, of course, completely nuts from the start."

As long as the South was solidly Democratic, the two political parties remained broad coalitions. The Democrats were a mixture of conservative Southerners and urban Northerners (both groups supported Franklin Roosevelt's populist economic activism, but they agreed on little else); the Republicans represented Wall Street and Main Street, the Eastern elite and the Western middle class (who agreed on a preference for limited government, and little else). In the 1950s and the first half of the 1960s, the Southern Democrats—who controlled, by seniority, many of the most important congressional committees—joined with the Republicans to prevent much of anything from happening except appropriations for highways and defense.

But the solid South shattered over civil rights. When Northern Democrats decided to support desegregation, a new generation of Southerners emerged and, during the next two decades, became Republicans. At the same time, many of the liberal children of the Eastern Republican elites joined the Democrats, as did Southern blacks when they gained the right to vote. As the parties became more ideologically "responsible," debate became more abrasive and partisan. In the House of Representatives, Democrats—stoked by moral outrage over segregation, Vietnam, and Watergate, and made complacent by their seemingly permanent majority—became far less tolerant of the Republican minority. The musty, ornate rituals of collegiality, the respectful parliamentary language, the staff and privileges granted the minority, were gradually abandoned or severely modified to the Republicans' disadvantage.

Tip O'Neill had his revenge against Gingrich and the Republicans during an outrageous episode in 1985. A very close congressional race in Indiana, between the Republican Rick McIntyre and the Democrat Frank McCloskey, had been decided, in a recount, in favor of McIntyre by Indiana's Republican Secretary of State; McCloskey protested to the House of Representatives, which decided to investigate. O'Neill chose a three-member commission, composed of two Democrats and a Republican. Not surprisingly, the Democrats voted to seat McCloskey—and the entire Republican caucus walked out of the House chamber in protest. "That was Newt's second big victory," Vin Weber said. "People began to think, 'Well, if the Democrats are going to be like that, maybe Newt's right. We might as well blow up the place.'"

Gingrich, empowered, continued his guerrilla warfare. In 1987, he brought ethics charges against Jim Wright, O'Neill's successor as Speaker of the House. The charges were flimsy and confusing at best: Wright was guilty of fairly standard political shenanigans—selling mass copies of a book he had written to lobbyists, a slightly too cozy relationship with a local business-man—and most members of Congress believed that Gingrich's campaign would be no more than a minor form of harassment. But the Wright case had an unanticipated aspect that raised the ante considerably and exacerbated the war between the parties: The House Ethics Committee appointed a Special Counsel, a Chicago Democrat named Richard Phelan, to investigate Wright. A year later, Phelan was still digging—this was an early indication of what might be called the Inspector Javert phenom-enon: the tendency of special prosecutors to become obsessed (as did Javert in *Les Misérables*), to slip the leash and expand their investigations well beyond the initial inquiry, to run up huge bills digging into every area of their target's life—and Wright was forced to resign. "I was worn out, completely spent," Wright told me later. "I couldn't sleep. I could see this thing dragging on another year or two and costing me a million dollars. I couldn't afford that. I gave a speech denouncing the 'mindless cannibal-ism' that was consuming the Congress and I figured my resigna-tion would so shock and shame the members that they'd end the war. That turned out to be a miscalculation on my part, of course. Things only got worse."

BY 1989, WHEN WRIGHT RESIGNED, it was clear that the ethics war had reached a new level of intensity. Each side was using high-powered legal weapons to stalk the other. The weapons were of recent vintage—the product of the historic government reform effort that came after the Watergate scandal. "We were going to reform the system," said Joseph Biden, referring to his generation's arrival in Congress. "But we created more problems than we solved. The campaign finance laws, the Independent Counsel statute—nothing turned out the way it was supposed to."

Biden might have added: the Ethics in Government Act of 1978; the reforms of the presidential-primary selection process and of the seniority system in Congress; the limitations on presidential war and budgetary powers; the "whistle-blower" reforms that enabled disgruntled government employees everywhere to bring anonymous complaints against their bosses; and the establishment of independent Inspectors General (a frightening, Javertian title) to process the whistle-blower complaints—a forest of new regulations that sprouted in the years after Watergate. Much of this was the work of the forty-three additional Democrats elected to the House in 1974, the first major infusion of Baby Boom politicians into the Congress. "They came to Congress wanting to end the war in Vietnam," said Jim Thurber, a political scientist at American University who served as an aide to Hubert Humphrey in the 1970s. But the war ended four months after they arrived "and the question was, what else could they do? One thing they all agreed upon was the need to reform the government."

Unquestionably, the reforms curtailed some outrageous practices—but the powerful new ethics weapons could easily be appropriated for trivial, partisan political use: The first investigation under the Independent Counsel statute, in 1979, was of

Jimmy Carter's chief of staff, Hamilton Jordan, for alleged cocaine use. The second was of Carter's campaign manager, Timothy Kraft, also for alleged cocaine use. No charges were filed in either case. When Ronald Reagan came to power, the Democrats returned the favor by investigating Labor Secretary Raymond Donovan, Attorney General Edwin Meese and the presidential aides Michael Deaver and Lyn Nofziger—with only Deaver eventually pleading guilty to an unrelated infraction. When Donovan was finally cleared after a grueling (and extremely expensive) investigation, he asked the memorable question, "Which office do I go to to get my reputation back?"

Indeed, the only Reagan-era investigation that transcended political pettiness had to do with the Iran–Contra scandal—the plan to sell arms illegally to Iran and use the proceeds to fund anti-Communist Nicaraguan rebels—and that case had a serious Javert component: The special prosecutor, Lawrence Walsh, remained in business four years after Reagan left office, and announced indictments just a few days before the 1992 presidential election, indictments that George H.W. Bush believed helped cinch the election for Bill Clinton. (Bush was not indicted—the former Defense Secretary Caspar Weinberger was— but, as Reagan's Vice President, Bush was peripherally involved. After he lost the election, he pardoned Weinberger.)

ALONG WITH THE POST-WATERGATE political reforms came an army of political reformers and a new industry: the Ethics Establishment. "I remember working as a congressional aide in the late sixties," said Norman Ornstein, a resident scholar at the American Enterprise Institute. "Across the street from our office was a building—the Methodist Building—that was filled with antiwar activists. And I remember thinking, 'What are these people going to do when the war is over?' They had learned a skill—political organizing—and they proceeded to put it to use. There was an explosion of 'public interest' activist groups in the early seventies, and they had a significant impact not just on political reforms, but also on environmental and consumer regulations. Then, in the late seventies, there was an explosion of industry groups and trade associations to counter-act them."

The various interest groups exerted a centrifugal pull on the Democrats and the Republicans, moving them to their respective extremes, where the most passionate advocates were festering. The trade associations formed political action committees, which brought enormous amounts of money into the system—especially after the Federal Election Campaign Act was amended, in 1979, to permit unlimited contributions to the national political parties (which was the origin of "soft" money, as opposed to the "hard" money contributed to specific candidates). The money was used to pay for advertising on television, which expanded in frequency and ferocity as the 1980s began. For many Democrats, the "war" actually began in 1980, when the National Conservative Political Action Committee (NC-PAC) ran a scurrilous television campaign against six liberal senators, four of whom were defeated—which returned control of the Senate to Republicans for the first time in twenty-six years. "You can't underestimate the impact that the rise of vicious, false, distorted negative advertising had on the members of Congress," said Warren Rudman, a Republican who left the Congress in disgust in 1992. "For example, I had a hard time getting to like Joe Lieberman when he came to the Senate, because the campaign he ran against Lowell Weicker, who was a good friend of mine, was disgraceful. Eventually, we became friendly, because Joe's a terrific guy. But a lot of people don't get over those things. It makes it a lot harder to work together—a lot harder to do anything. You're always wondering whether this or that vote is going to be distorted in some crummy ad in the next campaign."

If Democrats could point to NCPAC and Gingrich as the root causes of the incivility, Republicans were infuriated by the liberal activists' campaign in 1987 against the nomination of Robert Bork to the Supreme Court—and they were particularly enraged by the hyperbolic speech that Ted Kennedy made on the floor of the Senate less than an hour after the nomination had been announced. Kennedy ranted about a pandemic of terrible things, like "back-alley abortions," that would overwhelm "Robert Bork's America."

Alan Simpson, a Republican who served in the Senate from Wyoming and was the rarest of cats—a senator with a self-deprecating sense of humor—recalled: "All of us sort of stunned our colleagues by going off the deep end at one point or another during one of these circuses. Teddy did it with his Bork speech. Sam Nunn did it with his campaign against John Tower. I did it with Clarence Thomas, when I went ballistic over this 'sexual harassment' crap. I'll tell you, you get so wrapped up in the moment your mind sometimes comes unhinged."

The anti-Bork campaign and hearings almost seem decorous

compared with the crude personal assaults that came to charac-
terize later witch hunts. Bork was a distinguished academic but
an ideological bomb-thrower; an argument could be made that
he was not merely a conservative but a radical reactionary who
sought to overturn many of the precedents set by the liberal
Warren court. The leaders of the anti-Bork coalition decided to
have that argument made substantively, by constitutional schol-
ars, rather than emotionally; activists like Ralph Nader and
Molly Yard, of the National Organization for Women, were per-
suaded not to testify. Nader did meet with Joseph Biden, the
chairman of the Judiciary Committee, before the hearings began
and said that the Bork nomination, if handled correctly, could
be a "constituency-building exercise" for the liberal activists—
that is, a major direct mail fund-raising opportunity. Biden was
disgusted. "I told him no," he recalled, "and I'm proud of the
way those hearings were run."

Ralph Nader's personal asceticism and low-key style masked a
sour and unrelenting demagogue—and he clearly understood
the new political terrain better than Biden did. Indeed, Nader's
zealously anticorporate (and prolitigation) "Public Citizen" operation was a model widely admired by conservative activists.
The Bork nomination was the first time that a coalition of ideologues had mounted an activist campaign—including grassroots
organizing, opposition research, and even a television commer-
cial (featuring the voice of Gregory Peck)—to oppose a Supreme
Court appointment. This became a staple of the post-Bork prosecutorial scene, with activist groups using ethics targets, ranging
from Clarence Thomas to Bill Clinton, as a means of raising
"consciousness" and more important, money, from their sup-

porters. "One of the first things Ralph Nader taught me was to demonize the opposition," said Mike Pertschuk, a consumer advocate and Nader protégé, who wrote a book about the Bork campaign and who later, like Vin Weber, had mixed feelings about the harsh methods used. "It's a very effective tactic," he added. "But there's a terrible cost to that."

Another notable feature of the Bork campaign was the invasion of the nominee's privacy—particularly the attempt to investigate Bork's video store records by a reporter for the *Washington City Paper*, an alternative weekly. Only a few months earlier, reporters from the *Miami Herald* had waited in the bushes outside the townhouse of Gary Hart, a Democratic presidential candidate, to catch him in an adulterous liaison.

By now, the press had become an essential, omnivorous, and obnoxious component in the machinery of scandal. Bob Woodward and Carl Bernstein of the *Washington Post* had been the heroes of the Watergate episode. They had brought down a President. But that precedent caused a severe distortion in the culture of journalism—a new generation of reporters and editors were obsessed with replicating the *Post*'s feat during the Clinton presidency, but unlike Woodward and Bernstein, they fixed on the personal lives of their prey (not just Clinton—Gingrich, Housing Secretary Henry Cisneros, Commerce Secretary Ron Brown, and Republican congressmen Henry Hyde and Robert Livingston, among many others, had their personal peccadillos exposed). There was a gleeful, voyeuristic quality to much of the reporting; politicians were now, routinely, presumed guilty—especially on the new, witlessly contentious television sound-bite shows: "Groups" and "Gangs" of journalists screaming at each other and making facile judgments about complicated issues (perhaps "journalists" would be more appropriate, since many of these para-commentators were either former party propagandists or peripheral newsroom sorts with a frightening, innate ability to glow and crackle on television).

There was considerable peer pressure to stay cynical: Reporters who wrote favorably about politicians were considered to be "in the tank." A negative story about a politician was the safest story. "Over the past two decades, political reporters have become more concerned with how *other* political reporters judge their work," said Bill Kovach, a curator of the Neiman Fellowship program at Harvard. "Not wanting to look soft leads to a negative spin: No matter what position is taken by a politician, the journalistic tendency is to examine it in a negative light—to emphasize political calculations rather than substance."

Tom Patterson, a professor at Harvard's Kennedy School of Government, had the numbers to support Kovach's analysis. In the 1960 election, three-quarters of the references to the candidates that could be characterized as positive or negative were positive; by the 1988 campaign, the proportion had shifted to 60 percent negative (and remained there for Clinton's two campaigns). At the same time, stories emphasizing conflict between politicians increased *300 percent* from the early seventies to the late eighties. "The Watergate investigative model was very scrupulous," Patterson observed. "By the late seventies, that had changed—'investigative' reporting became getting on the phone and finding someone to attack someone else. The purpose wasn't to find things out but to bring politicians down."

The Natural

It is difficult to overstate the ire that most politicians, even those who had good relations with the press, began to feel toward journalists. "The media love hate," said Representative Barney Frank of Massachusetts, a homosexual whose private life was the subject of a breathless exposé in 1989. "In Washington, excessive cynicism is the most prevalent form of naïveté. I just wish reporters were as skeptical about bad news as they are about good news."

By 1989, the rigorous standards of Woodward and Bernstein's Watergate reporting—confirmation of a story by two independent sources, for example—had been long forgotten, even in the elite press. The enduring impact of George Bush's failed attempt to appoint the former Texas senator John Tower as his Defense Secretary was to take mainstream journalism to an ever more squalid level. The *Washington Post*, for example, published raw data from the FBI's investigation of Tower, including an unreliable account of two drinking-and-fondling incidents at an Air Force base—reported, as it happened, by Bob Woodward. The Tower case was bizarre and terrifying to many elected officials: no one could remember the last time a former senator had been denied a presidential appointment by his colleagues in the Senate. But Sam Nunn, Democrat of Georgia and a respected defense expert, was a very credible leader of the opposition, arguing that even the possibility of heavy drinking would be intolerable in a Secretary of Defense. "I liked Tower," Jim Wright later confided. "We were friends, fellow Texans, and I thought he had been treated unfairly. But it was clear, after that, that the Republicans were going to demand retribution. On Texas Independence Day, March 2, that year, a Republican told me the caucus was energized to come after me now. I said, 'What is this, an eye for an eye?' And he said, 'No, a Texan for a Texan.' "

Wright and Tower were both taken down in 1989. They had several other things in common: Neither was well liked by his colleagues, and neither had committed anything resembling a crime. "I disagreed with Newt about going after Wright," Vin Weber said. "In fact, Newt didn't have very much support at all in the Republican conference. But when Wright was forced to resign, that was Newt's third big triumph—and the Republican conference looked at Newt and said, 'He's been right all along.' "

ON MAY 15, 1984, THE DAY Newt Gingrich successfully confronted Tip O'Neill and received a standing ovation from his colleagues, one Republican did not join in the applause: Robert Michel of Peoria, Illinois, then House Minority Leader. Michel was, in many ways, Gingrich's opposite. He had grown up poor, the son of an immigrant factory worker (Gingrich, like Clinton, was from the low end of the middle class and the product of a broken home). After Pearl Harbor, Michel joined the infantry, rose to the rank of sergeant, and was seriously wounded in the Battle of the Bulge (Gingrich, like Clinton, managed to avoid service in Vietnam). When Michel was first elected to the House in 1956, he had a mission that he believed was the essence of conservatism: He wanted to give his fellow GIs and their families a period of peace and quiet. He wanted government kept under wraps; his goal was stability.

The Natural

"I still think I had a more conservative record than Newt," Michel told me in late 1998, after Gingrich had left Congress. He spoke slowly, his voice deep and pleasant and unpretentiously mid-American. "The media called me a 'moderate' because I talked with Democrats, but that was the way things were when I was coming up. Those were happy days. My district included Hiram Walker's distillery. A lot of members would come by the office for a snort, and we'd gas about this and that. When we had committee meetings, we'd sit at long tables, the majority and minority across from one another, and so we'd have to talk and work things out. Now they have those long daises, with the majority on one side and the minority way over on the other, and no one gets to know one another."

Newt Gingrich arrived in 1979, a Pennsylvanian transplanted to Georgia, a college professor and political activist who had only read about the wartime horrors that Bob Michel had experienced. Gingrich was obsessed with books about military tactics. He had become something of a reverse Clausewitz: He considered politics the extension of war by other means. "War without blood," he called it. Michel was appalled. He knew that politics was quite the opposite of war—it was the way you *avoided* war. "I don't think you can underestimate the generational aspect of this situation," said Vin Weber. "Our generation came in and we had absolutely no respect for any of the traditions—not the speakership, not the presidency, not bipartisanship. We thought the parliamentary language was stuffy and silly. We thought hypocrisy was the only sin. Bob Michel's generation—they wanted to make life less political for the returning veterans. We wanted to politicize everything. Remember the slogan, 'The personal is political'? That was the feminists, right? Well, that became us, too."

In the early 1990s, both the Gingrich Republicans and the feminists had their moments. The 1991 campaign against Clarence Thomas's nomination to the Supreme Court was far more personal and extreme than the campaign against Robert Bork had been. Members of the civil rights establishment set the tone by calling Thomas a variety of despicable names because he disagreed with the prevailing wisdom about affirmative action. Then the feminists had their moment with the sudden and belated appearance of Anita Hill, who accused Thomas of offensive ribaldry when he was boss at the Equal Employment Opportunity Commission; she was questioned intensely and skeptically by Alan Simpson and several other Republicans on the Judiciary Committee. A delegation of feminists visited Joseph Biden, just as Ralph Nader had done four years earlier. "They wanted the committee to expose the fact that Thomas watched pornographic films," Biden recalled. "But I told them that if he did, it wasn't material. It was private." (Of course, the media were happy to provide all the relevant details to a soap opera–loving public.) The incredible ugliness that both Thomas and Hill were forced to suffer—the grotesque invasion of their personal lives—was becoming part of the price paid by public servants. Any future presidential nominee could expect to have his or her closet emptied—as Zoe Baird and Kimba Wood, Clinton's first two nominees for Attorney General, soon would (for alleged improprieties associated with the hiring of immigrant baby-sitters). Indeed, a growing number of good people were deciding not to enter the public arena—and a growing number of politicians, particularly moderate sorts, were choosing to leave. A businessman who had declined Clinton's offer of a Cabinet position told me, "And go through *that*? What do I need that for?"

Meanwhile, Gingrich's demolition work in the House proceeded apace. The end of the Cold War meant that political anarchy could flourish in placid times. In the early nineties, hundreds of congressmen were tainted by their misuse of the House bank and post office (the latter operation resulted in a jail term for Dan Rostenkowski, the chairman of the House Ways and Means Committee); even the prices charged by the House barbershop were called into question. At the same time, Gingrich expanded his operation and took on his President, George Bush. In 1990, when Bush broke his "no new taxes" pledge by cutting a budget deal with the Democrats, Gingrich led a Republican revolt that forced a renegotiation of the deal—the first sign that a weakened Bush might not be invincible in the 1992 elections (the need to prevent similar right-wing betrayals was a lesson that George W. Bush carried with him to the presidency eight years later).

Bob Michel, who had supported the Bush budget deal, knew that he was going to be Gingrich's next target. "I could sense what was happening behind my back," Michel recalled. "Newt was coming along. He was going to challenge me for the leadership in 1994. It would have been a bitter challenge." He paused a moment. "I might have lost. I decided that I'd had enough. . . . I'm so *happy* I'm out!"

With Bush gone and Michel about to leave, Gingrich was ready—at the beginning of 1994—to turn his full attention toward Bill Clinton. And so was the press.

———

THE CLINTONS ARRIVED IN Washington with a cramped, defensive obsession with the forces arrayed against them. This tendency was encouraged by a truly odd, almost Shakespearean retinue of personal advisors—the First Lady always seemed to keep one such about, from her friend Susan Thomases to the former journalist Sidney Blumenthal—who earned their keep by floating vast, obscure, Manichean fantasies about the world outside the gates. (Blumenthal, called "Grassy Knoll" within the White House because of his conspiracy fetish, was widely reported to be famous for his chart of the Great Right-Wing Conspiracy to unseat the Clintons; he now claims it never existed.) The additional presence of a fair number of Little Rock political cronies—many of them former law partners of the First Lady—was neither unusual nor unwarranted, but it did nothing to diminish the garrison atmosphere.

Relations with the press had soured during the 1992 campaign and never improved. At the Inaugural Gala in 1993, a video was shown—produced by Clinton's Hollywood friends, Harry and Linda Thomasson—that featured prominent journalists making fools of themselves, predicting Clinton's demise during the campaign ("He's dead meat!"). To be sure, there were enemies out there—and powerful ones. A particularly vicious campaign was waged against Clinton by Robert Bartley of *The Wall Street Journal* editorial page, who assumed corruption from the very beginning. The centerpiece was a series of editorials questioning the integrity of the members of the Rose law firm in Little Rock who had come from Arkansas to join the Adminis-

———

tration—"Who is Webster Hubbell?" and then, "Who is Vincent Foster?" and then, "Who is William Kennedy III?" and ultimately, "Who is Hillary Clinton?" Foster mentioned the *Journal* screeds in anguished musings he had written on a yellow legal pad, and then torn to pieces, before he committed suicide on July 13, 1993.

Foster's suicide intensified the battle between the President and the press. For the Clintons, the message was clear: This was to be, literally, war to the death. At the same time, Foster's death reinforced the fantasy of a lethal immorality about the Clintons (at least, among the more hydrophobic and deluded sensationalists in the press, who spread the notion that Foster had been murdered). Two separate investigations by special prosecutors would be required to confirm the obvious: that Foster had taken his own life.

The Clintons were particularly infuriated by the willingness of responsible journalists to sell wholesale what irresponsible Clinton-haters were peddling retail. The most significant of these was an article in the combative, if often juvenile, conservative magazine, the *American Spectator*, in which former Arkansas state troopers told tales about the sex lives of the former governor and First Lady. (The investigation was funded by the conservative billionaire, Richard Mellon Scaife, whose name was prominent on Blumenthal's Right-Wing Conspiracy chart.) The *Los Angeles Times*, which had also been interviewing troopers, quickly printed its version of the story, which was then picked up by everyone else. Indeed, "Troopergate"—it was soon immortalized with the banal journalistic ritual of a "-gate" suffix—began the process that would lead to the impeachment of the

President. One of Clinton's alleged women, Paula Jones, was encouraged by conservatives to come forward and tell her story: that the governor of Arkansas had approached her in a gross manner and she had refused him vehemently. The trooper who had originally told this story, Danny Ferguson, had a different version: Jones had visited Clinton in a hotel room and emerged smiling, offering herself in perpetuity as "the governor's girlfriend."

The Paula Jones story was dismissed at first, mostly because of its ideological provenance. But it had the ring of truth—at least, Ferguson's version did—and it gained great, if initially surreptitious, currency in Washington. I was among the earliest in the mainstream press to make a big deal of it, in precisely the way the Clintons found most reprehensible—metaphorically, and somewhat disingenuously. In a May 1994 *Newsweek* essay entitled "The Politics of Promiscuity," I argued that Clinton's tendency toward sloppy policy-making, particularly overseas, might be a reflection of his sloppy personal habits. The argument soon was proved wrong-headed (to its author, at least) as the President gradually became far more disciplined in his statements and public actions, but the theory became a staple of the conservative case against Clinton, especially during the Lewinsky scandal.

By the end of 1993, relations between the Clintons and their various opponents were rapidly deteriorating. The *Washington Post* was demanding documents from the Clintons relating to the Whitewater land deal. This was an impenetrable nonstory, with some irresistible elements to it: The Clintons had entered into a real estate venture, arguably a sweetheart deal in which their potential for loss was minimized (although the proposition was so goofy that they did eventually lose some money) with some shady characters who were simultaneously looting a local savings and loan institution. Indeed, the central players in the Whitewater affair—Jim and Susan McDougal—provided further evidence of the Clintons' spotty taste in friends and business associates. There was also the "appearance of impropriety" in other business dealings during the Arkansas years: The First Lady had made a great deal of money with very little risk dealing in hog futures. But, after years of dedicated investigation, and the expenditure of $50 million in public funds for a special prosecutor, absolutely no evidence of criminality would ever be found.

"I had a fascinating conversation with one of the Republican senators in the middle of the D'Amato hearings," Clinton later told me, referring to the Senate Whitewater hearings chaired by Senator Alfonse D'Amato of New York. "They were impugning Hillary and I asked this guy, 'Do you really think my wife and I did anything wrong in this Whitewater thing?' He just started laughing. He said, 'Of course you didn't do anything wrong. That's not the point. The point of this is to make people think you did something wrong.' "

In other words, the initial Clinton scandals were not a unique or discrete phenomenon, but an integral part of the ethics war, the Gingrichization of politics that had been escalating for twenty years; it was the latest iteration of the Jim Wright and John Tower prosecutions. The press was playing its assigned role as well. "That same senator also said the Republicans learned a lot from my presidency," Clinton added. "He said that before, they thought the press was liberal, but 'now we have a different view. We think they're liberal and they vote like you, but they think like us and that's more important.' I said, 'What do you mean?' And he said, 'Well, we just don't believe in government very much, but we love power and, you know, the press wants to be powerful and we both get it the same way—by hurting you.' I mean, there could be something to that. Maybe there were times when I didn't handle the press all that well in the early days, but . . . if you look back over it, the Whitewater thing was a total fraud."

This rather convenient conversation with the unnamed senator may or may not be mythical—the press, mindless beast that it has become, is more interested in sensational stories than it is in power—but it is a very good indication of the President's sense of the Washington battlefield: The First Lady wasn't the only one who believed in conspiracies. Clinton was right about the insubstantiality of most of the charges thrown against him, but his response to the scandal-mongering was a furious, self-defeating defiance that overwhelmed his White House and limited his ability to enact the grander goals of his presidency.

Indeed, the *Washington Post*'s initial request for Whitewater information led to a turning point in the history of the Administration—a rare moment when even George Stephanopoulos and David Gergen agreed on the proper course of action: release everything, answer every question, lance the wound. The President and the First Lady disagreed, vehemently. In his memoir, *All Too Human*, Stephanopoulos described a meeting in the Oval Office on December 11, 1993, in which he and Gergen pleaded with the President to relent:

"I don't have a big problem with giving them what we have," he said, almost apologetically, his mind elsewhere. . . . "But Hillary . . ."

Saying her name flipped a switch in his head. Suddenly, his eyes lit up and two years worth of venom spewed out of his mouth. You could easily tell when Clinton was making Hillary's argument: Even if he was yelling, his voice had a flat quality, as if he were a high school debater speeding through a series of memorized facts. That antipress script was familiar to me by now. "No, you're wrong," he said. "The questions *won't* stop. . . . They'll *always* want more. *No* president has ever been treated the way I've been treated."

More than six years later, when I asked Clinton if the decision to refuse the *Washington Post* had been a mistake, he responded in much the same manner as Stephanopoulos had described, but now he added additional targets: unnamed staff members—Gergen and Stephanopoulos, no doubt—who'd counseled him to cooperate. He began quietly, saying he didn't believe cooperating with the *Post* would have made any difference in the end. "What I regret," he said, "is asking for a special counsel."

Clinton had asked Attorney General Janet Reno to appoint someone to investigate the Whitewater matter in January 1994. She chose a moderate Republican, Robert Fiske, who was later replaced—when a federal court intervened—by Kenneth Starr. The President's eyes narrowed and his jaw clenched as he remembered asking Reno to act: "I did it because I was exhausted, because I had just buried my mother, and because I had people in the White House who couldn't stand the heat and they suggested that I do it, that I had to do it. I knew there was nothing to it, it was just a lie—and I had people like Bruce Lindsey and [White House Counsel] Bernie Nussbaum screaming at me not to do it. . . . I believe that the almost hysterical desire to have something to investigate was so great that it wouldn't have made any difference. Why did this thing hang on? There was nothing in those private papers. . . . And if you notice, when Starr got ahold of this, he immediately abandoned it and went on to other stuff. There never was anything to it . . . and I have no reason to believe that [giving the documents to the *Washington Post*] would have made any difference. I think they would have found some way to say, 'Oh, there are questions here. Let's have a special counsel.' "

Clinton is probably right about that. But Stephanopoulos and Gergen are also right: The rather combustible phenomenon at the heart of this fury was the relationship between the President and the First Lady.

CHAPTER
FIVE

The late Diane Blair, one of Hillary Rodham Clinton's closest friends, once told me a remarkable story about the Clinton marriage. On a visit to the White House, Blair was chatting with the First Lady in her study; it was a rambling conversation that eventually settled on the global warming treaty then being negotiated in Japan. Blair observed that "even intelligent people have trouble understanding what this is all about," and the First Lady agreed. The President then dropped in, joined the conversation, and soon, much to Blair's surprise, had launched into a furious argument with his wife. "They were arguing about whether it does any good to do the right thing on a controversial issue if no one has a clue you're doing it," Blair recalled (it would have been nice to know which Clinton was arguing which side, but Blair was too good a friend to reveal that). "It was a high-pitched argument. It would not have seemed, to most people, the picture of loveliness. They were really, really angry with each other. And then, suddenly, the President took her in his arms and started kissing her all over her face and he said, 'God, what would I do without you!' I felt kind of embarrassed being there—I wanted to leave the room. But I just don't think you can fake that sort of thing."

There are several plausible ways to react to this story. One is "Oh, yuck." Another is "Oh, come on." A cynic might say Blair was an old friend—and the wife of Jim Blair, the Tyson Foods lawyer who was involved with Mrs. Clinton in the controversial hog futures trading—and that she was cleverly perpetuating the party line that this was a solid, loving marriage: a real relationship, not a political arrangement. There was a third possible reaction, though. Blair's story conformed to the recollections of a great many people who knew the Clintons well, even some who had left their employ feeling betrayed and disheartened. (And some independent observers as well: I accidentally witnessed the Clintons in a serious snuggle on a dark pathway after a campaign speech in Columbia, South Carolina, in 1992.)

The quality and texture, and the nature, of the Clinton marriage was the great abiding mystery of his presidency. Unlike most inquiries into the private lives of politicians, this one was legitimate—because of the First Lady's deep and obvious involvement in the formulation of public policy (as opposed to the President's apparent weakness for involvements of other sorts). Most of the speculation was vapid, tabloidy stuff. If he strayed so egregiously and she stayed around, it must have been a cold, political partnership—her control of health care policy, for example, was often described as a quid pro quo for keeping the public illusion of a marriage alive. Other strands of speculation were woven from psychobabble about "enablers" and "addicts" and "denial." But even the best marriages are tangled and contradictory affairs, their psychological terrain unknowable to all but the immediate participants. "The only people who count in any marriage are the two that are in it," the First Lady would say on NBC's *Today* program, at the beginning of the Lewinsky scandal. She had made similar comments during the Gennifer Flowers scandal in 1992. "We know everything there is to know about each other, and we understand and accept and love each other." (As it happened, Mrs. Clinton, at that moment, didn't quite know all there was to know about Monica Lewinsky.)

Over time, I decided that the wisest course regarding the Clinton marriage was to be indiscriminately credulous, to believe *all* the stories: He was chronically unfaithful. They fought like harpies. They were political partners. They were best friends. They loved each other madly, in every sense of the word. None of these were mutually exclusive. A photograph of the Clintons in bathing suits, dancing together, on a beach at St. Thomas as the Paula Jones lawsuit gained steam could serve as a laboratory for the theory of indiscriminate credulity. No doubt they were aware of the cameras, even though the photographers were distant and surreptitious—the inevitable White House protest about the invasion of their privacy was laughable—and they probably knew that the image might serve as a mild antidote to the embarrassment of the Jones lawsuit. But it is also not impossible, and not at all contradictory, that the Clintons were quite besotted with each other at that moment. The President's problem never was a deficiency of affection. And, as for the First Lady, a friend said, "I think she's goofy about him."

Which is not to say that it wasn't a stupefyingly weird relationship. There were public aspects of the marriage that were confusing, to say the least. Why, for example, did Hillary Clinton always look so radiant in the midst of one of her husband's sex scandals? (Well, not always—she looked tired when she defended her husband and announced the "great right-wing conspiracy" on the *Today* show at the beginning of the Lewinsky ordeal; and she looked taut, devastated, at the end—when he finally admitted to the nation, and to her, that he had lied about it.) Staff members recalled a moment during the New Hampshire primary in 1992, when the Gennifer Flowers and draft evasion scandals were raging. "We were all completely depressed and totally scruffy, the hotel we were staying in was a mess," Mandy Grunwald, a media advisor in the campaign, recalled, "and she walked in one morning dressed to the nines. It was a dark pants suit with brass buttons, I think. She had her makeup on, her hair was done meticulously. She had done all this intentionally, to send us a message: 'Stop moping! We're going to be professionals. The worse you feel, the better you should look.' It was her way of getting us going again."

Another theory regarding the First Lady's radiance was less charitable. She looked good because she was invigorated by crises. Her husband needed her desperately at such times; she was the essential element in his defense. Some Clinton acquaintances saw this as a matter of love and insecurity: The First Lady was eager to win the President's affection whenever, and however, she could. A less friendly interpretation, from some staff members, was that it was a matter of power: If he was in her debt for defending him, she had more power to pursue her staffing and policy objectives. Again, none of these explanations were mutually exclusive. And it is also not unreasonable to observe that despite, and sometimes because of, the complexities of their marriage, the Clintons tended toward a united, myopic, defensive irrationality in moments of stress.

"You have to realize that the President always saw her as magic politically," a former staff member said. "He thought she had the magic touch." Several members of the campaign staff remembered a meeting in early July 1992, when the Clinton team was brainstorming his Democratic National Convention acceptance speech. Mrs. Clinton was the one who came up with the last line—"I still believe in a place called Hope"—and, Mandy Grunwald recalled, "the look he gave her at that moment was unforgettable. It was like, 'You *always* know that right thing.' "

This may help account for the President's strange, and utterly disastrous, decision to bequeath health insurance reform—the issue that he hoped would be the most important legacy of his administration, and which certainly stands as his greatest policy failure—to the First Lady. The health issue reached its critical stage at the very same moment, in early 1994, that the press became obsessed with Whitewater and the Trooper Tales. Certainly, the impolitic stubbornness of the Clintons in the handling of the health issue—their refusal to compromise until it was too late—seemed more in keeping with the First Lady's style than with the President's.

It was an odd style, at once secretive and candid and vehement. Hillary Rodham Clinton is very much a Methodist of the straight-laced, moralizing, nineteenth-century sort (her husband is very much an emotive Baptist); in another time, she might have been an abolitionist, a suffragist, or a founder of the Women's Christian Temperance Union. She established, and was a fanatic enforcer of, the no-smoking rules in the White House; when she traveled, her plane offered only the austere, "heart-healthy," high-fiber cuisine touted by her friend, Dr. Dean Ornish. She was said to be warm and generous and hilarious in private, but she was odd in public—she seemed to feel the need to be perfect, when merely being human would have sufficed.

She inspired an almost fanatic loyalty among her staff, most of whom were women who saw her as an iconic figure, even though she clearly intimidated them (several denizens of Hillaryland, as her staff called itself, suffered from Tippi Hedren Syndrome: They looked as if they were about to be attacked by birds). But none of them ever wrote a tell-all memoir about the boss. "Two important things you should know about Mrs. Clinton," said James Carville. "She never forgot her family. Her father died two blocks from the state capitol in Little Rock. And no one on her staff ever betrayed her. That's all you need to know about her character."

"She's unvarnished. She said what she thought," recalled Bruce Reed, who served as the President's domestic policy advisor (a difficult position, since most people assumed that Mrs. Clinton was the President's real domestic policy advisor). The President, always the public softie, dreaded delivering bad news to the staff; the First Lady had no such qualms. "She never cared what people thought of her," Reed added. "She didn't need people to like her."

The politics of Hillaryland was a bit more complicated than the paleo-liberalism assumed, and broadcast, by conservatives.

Indeed, the First Lady's politics was very similar to that of the Gang of Four—the political consultants who worked the 1992 campaign. She was, and remains, a social conservative and an economic liberal. But she was not very diplomatic about it. Her Methodist vehemence led to a disastrous inflexibility on health care. "She was far more suspicious of concentrated power, corporate power, than the President was," Reed recalled. "This was true even before health care. But the television campaign that the insurance industry ran against her—the 'Harry and Louise' ads—iced the cake."

THE HEALTH INSURANCE FIASCO involved two related failures: a substantive failure and a political one. The substantive failure had to do with the plan that emerged from the Health Care Task Force led by Mrs. Clinton and Ira Magaziner: It was intended as the simplest, most direct path to universal coverage, a mere extension of the messy American status quo—all employers would be required to provide health insurance for their employees. This "employer mandate" aroused intense opposition from the small-business community and its Republican friends in Congress, of course. But it was also an odd position for Bill Clinton to be taking, more of an Old than a New Democrat solution. The plan was cluttered with ancillary details: In order to "prove" that the new system would not bust the budget, a ridiculously detailed proposal was written, which specified the sort of coverage employers would have to provide and also created a complicated bureaucracy to make sure that health care costs remained in control. "Most people in the *White*

House couldn't understand what was in the plan," said a high-ranking staff member with congressional experience. "If they couldn't explain it to us, they weren't going to explain it to the Congress."

Magaziner says in retrospect, and with some justification, that the health care plan was allowed to become as ornate as it did because he wasn't provided with the political and legislative experts necessary to show him the limits of the possible. "The battle to pass the budget was so intense," he recalled, "that no one was ever available to help out. I had a meeting in March 1993 with the House leadership, including several of the Democratic Committee chairs—tough, smart guys like Dan Rostenkowski and John Dingell. Howard Paster [Clinton's congressional liaison] was supposed to go with me, to explain the legislative strategy. But he was pulled into a budget meeting. And so, after I did my part and explained the plan, Rostenkowski looked at me and said, 'Okay, now how are we going to get this done?' And, of course, I had no idea. Two hours later, Howard gets a phone call from Rosty, 'What the hell is this?' I never had credibility with them again."

But others remember a less humble Magaziner and an adamant First Lady. Magaziner was a former student radical—he had forced, and then supervised, the renovation of the undergraduate curriculum at his alma mater, Brown University—who became a successful management consultant and seemed to combine the worst attributes of the two: a need for theoretical purity and a tendency to overmanage. The workings of the health care task force were secret. A know-it-all smugness became the operational style; "incrementalists" were scorned (and the definition of an "incrementalist" was anyone who didn't buy, in its entirety, a 1,300-page piece of legislation that redesigned one seventh of the American economy and then encrusted it with a swath of new rules and regulations). Within the White House itself, the same disastrous scene was played out, over and over, in the months before the plan was made public: Magaziner and Mrs. Clinton would give a progress report; questions would be raised; the First Lady would, with cold fury, tell the questioner to stuff it—their plan was *the* plan. It was the right thing to do. They were going to do it. The President sat quietly through these sessions as the First Lady bludgeoned respected members of the Administration—like Lloyd Bentsen, Bob Rubin, and Leon Panetta—into silence (as well as not-so-respected members like David Gergen). "I remember the first time I heard them lay it out," Panetta recalled. "My reaction was, this is impossibly complicated. The First Lady did what she always did— she acted as if anyone who disagreed with her didn't know what they were talking about—and I said to myself, 'Okay, I'm recusing myself from this issue.' "

The President later admitted, during one of our conversations, that a more elegant, Third Way solution would have been to simply give health care tax credits (or vouchers, in effect) to those who needed them, mostly the working poor (the very poorest people receive health care coverage through Medicaid). This was, essentially, the proposal first made by Stuart Butler of the Heritage Foundation and resurrected, in modified form, by former senator Bill Bradley in the 2000 Democratic presidential primary campaign. "That's what you're going to have to do eventually," the President conceded, "and if I could do it now, that's what I would offer. The problem was, I couldn't do it in ninety-four, with the deficits the way they were, without a tax increase."

But there was a plan in 1994—a Republican plan, proposed by Senator John Chafee of Rhode Island—that approached universal coverage through an "individual mandate" (which is to say, a tax credit system of the sort favored by Butler and Bradley). It even included a tax increase to help pay for it. Furthermore, the Chafee plan, introduced in broad outline the week after Clinton's gargantuan proposal, had twenty-four Republican cosponsors, including then Senate Minority Leader Bob Dole. Years later, I asked Clinton what would have happened if he, or the First Lady, had rushed over to Chafee's press conference, dumped the task force's 1,300-page bill in the wastebasket, and said, "I'm with him."

"Maybe if I'd gone to Chafee's press conference, that would have worked," the President said, reluctantly. But both he and the First Lady were convinced that Dole—who was thinking about running for President in 1996 and was always concerned about his credibility with the Republican right (especially after Gingrich unseated Bob Michel)—would have been forced to back out eventually. The President said that he offered to work with Dole, to create a bipartisan health insurance plan. "And Dole said to me—I'll never forget this because we were at a joint leadership meeting in the Cabinet Room—he said, 'No, that's not the way we should do it. You introduce a bill, we'll introduce a bill, and then we'll get together, and we'll pass a compromise.' Then Dole got a memo from Bill Kristol"—a Republican strategist who later became publisher of the conservative magazine the

Weekly Standard—"which basically took the Gingrich line: If universal health care passes, the Democrats will get credit for it. So you have to make sure that nothing happens. After that, I don't think we really had a chance. . . . With that single exception, in all my other dealings with Dole, he was always honest. In this case, I think he saw a chance to win the majority in Congress, a chance to get elected President . . . and that's what I think happened."

There is a cosmic accuracy to the President's recollection, but some problems with the specifics. Dole didn't remember the scene in the Cabinet Room (and Magaziner, and others, recalled Chafee—working on Dole's instructions, no doubt—making the offer of separate, partisan bills leading to a compromise). And there is evidence that Dole, a severely wounded World War II veteran whose life was saved by government-provided health care, wanted to find some sort of compromise. "We had several dinner meetings and I remember saying to the First Lady, 'If you can sell it to Sheila, you can probably sell it to me,' " Dole recalled, referring to his legislative assistant, Sheila Burke, who was very knowledgeable about health care issues. "Everyone knew there was a problem. There were all these children who needed coverage," Dole continued, "but we had no input. And, as I recall, Mrs. Clinton didn't want to give up very much—and then the opposition to *any* sort of plan did start building up within my party."

From the start, Daniel Patrick Moynihan—the chairman of the Senate Finance Committee, which is *the* essential committee when it comes to economic policy issues—had warned the Clintons that there was a unique ecology to the Senate: Big programs like universal health insurance either achieved a bipartisan consensus and passed with large majorities, seventy-five or eighty votes in favor, or they didn't pass at all. Moynihan's advice was ignored within the White House—at a February 1994 meeting of Democratic Committee chairs who were involved in the health care issue, he was the only pessimist. (Moynihan was assumed to be an enemy in any case, since he had supported Nebraska senator Bob Kerrey for the Democratic presidential nomination in 1992.) In any event, the zealotry emanating out of the Health Care Task Force, augmented by bad advice from some of the more liberal senators—and by a witless revulsion in Hillaryland to the "incrementalists" in the Senate who favored health insurance reform but believed that something less than universal coverage was the only possible deal to be had—defined the White House position. The zealots argued that Moynihan was wrong about the Senate ecosystem. The President had just won a huge Senate victory, on the 1993 budget plan, by a single vote. Health insurance could be jammed through the legislature in similar fashion. But the passage of an annual budget is a mandatory act, and passage of universal health insurance is not. The unwillingness to compromise until it was way too late proved fatal.

In January 1994, the President probably sealed the fate of the plan with a truly impolitic, and decidedly un-Clintonian, gesture in his State of the Union address: He pulled a pen from his pocket, waved it in the air, and promised to veto any health care bill that didn't provide universal coverage. Lawrence O'Donnell, Moynihan's chief of staff on the Finance Committee, believes that the histrionics were not accidental: "I had lunch with

Magaziner in the White House just before the speech," he recalled, "and I told him what was possible: We might be able to get a nonmandatory deal that would cover ninety or ninety-one percent of the people. He said, flatly, 'We'll veto that.' I'm convinced that he went to Clinton and said, 'Here's where they're headed and you've got to stop them.' And that's why he did the pen thing."

By the late spring of 1994, the President was beginning to understand that health care reform was comatose. His pollster, Stan Greenberg, told him that the Democrats might even have trouble retaining the Senate because of the public's sense of frustration over Congress's inability to act (there was, at this point, no way to see the historic cataclysm ahead, the loss of both houses of Congress to the Republicans). Greenberg had an idea: Withdraw the health plan and replace it with a welfare reform bill. If the Democrats could pass both welfare reform and a crime bill—which would provide funding for a hundred thousand more police officers—they'd have a record of accomplishment to run on in the fall elections. Clinton thought this was an interesting idea and he asked Greenberg to approach House Speaker Tom Foley about it. "Foley said absolutely not," Greenberg recalled. The liberals, especially the members of the black caucus, would be totally opposed to welfare reform. Foley believed there was still hope that a health care bill could be pushed through the House. And if it failed, the Republicans could be blamed for blocking a government program that even Greenberg's polls still indicated was popular with the public.

Foley and fifty-one other Democrats would lose their seats in the elections of 1994, relinquishing authority of the House of

Representatives to Newt Gingrich's Republicans for the first time in forty years (the Democrats lost ten Senate seats and control of that body as well). The causes of the Republican landslide are still debated, but central to their victory was the public's sense that Bill Clinton wasn't who he'd said he would be—that he was an old-fashioned liberal who hung out with Hollywood types, that he was more concerned with gay rights than with middle-class concerns, and that he had proposed a complicated, ridiculous, big-government program to address an issue, health insurance security, that a substantial majority of the public was truly worried about. The First Lady was a particular target; and, in retrospect, it seems fair to say that her inability to sense the political realities—her unwillingness, from the very start, to listen to opposing points of view in White House staff meetings, and then her unwillingness to compromise until it was too late—made the final result inevitable.

Clinton later acknowledged that the entire White House strategy was a mistake, that the First Lady's task force should only have produced a general statement of principles and then said, " 'Okay, here's all of our work . . . you guys draft the bill.' Or I should have insisted that we have a joint bill." But he refused to second-guess either his wife or the decision to put her in charge of so prominent a policy initiative. "She gets a total bum rap on this," he said. "She was told, we're not going to have a tax increase, but you have to get one hundred percent coverage. And she was told that managed care was coming, but you have to have some restraints"—all those complicated rules and regulations—"on it. So she was operating within constraints that we now know are impossible. . . . But it was my mistake, not hers. All she did was what she was asked to do."

IN THE SPRING OF 1995, I accompanied Mrs. Clinton on her first solo overseas trip—to South Asia, an excursion that also served as her reentry into public life after the health insurance disaster. It was a wonderful trip. Mrs. Clinton was charming. She and her daughter, Chelsea, spent an unusual amount of time in the back of the plane, chatting with the reporters (most of whom were women). These conversations were off the record and informal—at one point, Mrs. Clinton invited us forward to watch a video, and she greeted us wearing an old sweatshirt and Coke-bottle eyeglasses. Chelsea was poised and funny and smart; she had no reluctance about interrupting her mother—correcting her at times—when the two recounted the events of the day. Their relationship seemed refreshingly normal (a remarkable achievement, given the circumstances).

The intimacy with the press led to a difficult moment on the day we visited the Taj Mahal. An Associated Press reporter asked Chelsea, "Hey, what'd you think of it?" Chelsea's reply—she'd thought it was great—was on the international wires immediately, the first time (to my knowledge) that she'd ever been quoted during the Clinton presidency. The television correspondents were soon under pressure from their bosses back in the States: Had they gotten the Chelsea "interview" on film? When they approached the First Lady and asked if they could interview Chelsea about this, she snapped, "No, no!" and was hustled off by aides, leaving the reporters mystified by her sudden vehemence. The First Lady's insistence that their daughter not be used as media fodder, admirable in principle and uniformly respected by the press, suddenly seemed inflexible and dogmatic, a reminder of all that had gone wrong during the past year.

Margaret Carlson of *Time* magazine and I had a long conversation with Mrs. Clinton that night in New Delhi. She seemed to be reassessing her political philosophy after the health reform debacle. She was clearly impressed with the nongovernmental social programs she had been visiting—indeed, *all* the programs she visited on the subcontinent were nongovernmental—and she was beginning to wonder if the needs of poor women and children might best be served by circumventing the government bureaucracy (a classic New Democrat formulation). She was, as ever, cautious about this—"there are good and bad governmental programs and good and bad nongovernmental programs," she said (a classic Hillarian formulation)—but there was a curiosity and a humility that hadn't seemed apparent before.

In Pakistan, she met with a group of young women, children of the elite, at the Islamabad College for Women. The students, who sat in a circle surrounding the First Lady in a classroom cooled by electric fans on a very hot day, explained—eloquently, in a fashion that was even more moving because it was so dignified—that they were afraid that they wouldn't be able to achieve their ambitions in a country suddenly overtaken by a conservative brand of Islam (Pakistan's mullahs had been relatively moderate until the revolution, next door, in Iran). "We need to establish trust with the common people," said a young woman who hoped to go into advertising, "so they will understand we're not their enemies. They think that with education, girls will get out of hand."

"That's difficult to do sometimes—establish trust," the First Lady said, and then eased into what seemed almost a private rumination on mullahs, American and Asian. She talked about "the great struggle" to build a tolerant but still "spiritual" response to the "rampant materialism and consumerism . . . because many of those who are concerned about the lack of meaning and the undermining of family life would like to adopt a rigid response to it."

Her husband's battle against a rigid American mullah named Newt Gingrich would consume the next several years. It would prove successful; indeed, it will probably stand as a textbook example of how a tactically astute President can transform a position of weakness into strength. But that outcome was far from obvious in the spring of 1995, and Mrs. Clinton was very curious, privately, about Gingrich. They were the same, in a way: ideological lightning rods for opposition extremists. But they were different, too. Gingrich had had a difficult childhood. An army brat who had become an angry man, he embraced bombast, adored controversy, and was thrilled by the enemies his defiant, adolescent anger created. Hillary Clinton was perplexed by the strong feelings she aroused; she always had been mistrustful of certain aspects of public life—perhaps, simply, by the public ownership of her private life. After the health care episode, and after the deaths of her father and of her good friend Vince Foster, she seemed wounded and understandably depressed. In the second Clinton term, the wounds would only deepen, and so would the mysterious quality of her marriage.

———

AT THE END OF the conversation in which the President and I discussed the great health care disaster, Mrs. Clinton suddenly appeared and asked me, with a smile, how she had fared. "He ripped you up," I told her, also with a smile.

The President fairly leaped from his chair, crossed the room, put his arms around Mrs. Clinton, and kissed her several times on the forehead. "I told him," he said, hugging her tight, "that health care was all my fault."

CHAPTER
SIX

Leon Panetta has an easy laugh and a humble style that seems to radiate moderation. He also has an eclectic pedigree: a former Republican, he became a Democrat in the Nixon era, largely because of civil rights; he served in the Congress for sixteen years, a conservative on fiscal matters, but liberal on most everything else. In 1993, when Bill Clinton asked him to become the director of the Office of Management and Budget, Panetta was thrilled to be working for a President who, finally, shared his passion for fiscal discipline. But after eighteen months of White House chaos, the budget director was perplexed that so talented a politician would tolerate so much disorganization around him. He sensed that part of the problem was Clinton's innate Southern courtliness. "His nature is not to be confrontational. You watched the president and Al Gore talk about issues and it was very impressive, but the exact opposite of two Italians—so calm, so cordial! I never heard the President tell anyone, 'You're full of shit,' even when I knew he wanted to."

Mac McLarty, who had nominally presided over the mayhem of the first two years, was very much the same. Panetta believed that a screamer—a nice screamer—was desperately needed in some position of authority. On a trip to Europe in June 1994, the President asked the budget director for his opinion about White House operations—and got an earful about the need for a more seasoned, organized staff. Panetta was particularly exercised about the lingering presence of the 1992 political campaign consultants who were not members of the White House staff, but had security passes that gave them regular access to the West Wing. Their constant and very public involvement, Panetta believed, made every decision seem a political one. "We've got too many campaign types," Panetta told the President. "They're great at blowing up balloons, but you need people who know how to govern."

This may have been more clever than accurate. The campaign types were, at that point, sliding into disrepute. They had been responsible for the the selling of the health care plan, and they were easier to blame for the proposal's failure than the First Lady was. In any event, Panetta was soon summoned to Camp David and offered the job of chief of staff. He refused, at first; he told the President he was happy in his current job, and probably more valuable to the Administration as budget director. "Leon," the President said, "you could be the greatest budget director in history and no one will notice, if the White House is falling apart."

Soon Panetta found himself presiding over a more orderly,

but still extremely strange, West Wing operation. There were three matched pairs of advisors, only one of which was under the chief of staff's direct control. The First Lady and the Vice President were the senior pair—the First Lady was a bit more reticent and pragmatic after health care, but she was still the leading liberal voice in the operation, and Al Gore remained the most consistent New Democrat. Panetta added his own matched pair, two new deputy chiefs of staff: the liberal bulldog Harold Ickes, whose responsibilities were to handle the political aspects of the presidency, as well as the care and feeding of Democratic constituency groups; and Erskine Bowles, director of the Small Business Administration and a moderate, who took charge of organization and scheduling. The third pair of advisors was where things got really strange. One was Stephanopoulos, who had lost favor with the Clintons after it had become obvious that he was a primary source for Bob Woodward's book about the 1993 budget deal. But George now formed a close alliance with Panetta, providing him with tactical advice about how to handle the President and also how to deal with the new Republican majority in the Congress. And then there was . . . someone else—an advisor with direct access to the President whose identity was, at first, a mystery to Panetta and then, an outrage.

The mystery advisor was the political consultant Dick Morris, who had helped Clinton regain the governorship of Arkansas after his defeat in 1980. Morris was a prohibitively bizarre human being, a product of New York's steamy, overwrought Democratic politics. He and Harold Ickes had been rivals on the Upper West Side of Manhattan ever since their political infancies in the 1960s; and Ickes soon found himself in the uncomfortable position of raising huge amounts of money for Morris to spend on television advertising for Clinton's reelection campaign. Morris was brilliant, unpredictable, and a self-described quasi-autistic neurotic; he drove everyone around him crazy with his endless monologues and reflexive deviousness. It was said that Clinton had once slammed Morris against a wall in the governor's mansion, which may have been the only recorded instance of Bill Clinton making war, not love—but then, *everyone*, sooner or later, wanted to slam Morris up against a wall, including his wife, Elaine.

In recent years, Morris had become politically ambidextrous— one of his more prominent clients was Trent Lott, the new Republican Senate Majority Leader (he had also helped North Carolina's antediluvian Visigoth senator, Jesse Helms, run a loathsome reelection campaign). But that hadn't stopped the First Lady, who was as pragmatic about politics as she was idealistic about policy, from asking Morris for advice on how to save the presidency, just after the elections in November 1994. The First Lady and the political consultant also shared an odd proclivity for the surreptitious: Morris's existence was to be kept a secret. His code name was "Charlie," which may or may not have been a reference to the disembodied voice in the old *Charlie's Angels* television series. It was, Panetta believed, "weird . . . very weird."

Morris's presence, when it was eventually divulged, seemed further evidence of Clinton's lack of political scruple or philosophy. Again, the President had gone to an "outside" advisor in order to steer himself onto a more moderate path and again, like David Gergen, the advisor was sort of a Republican—which reinforced the notion, especially among liberals, that the "New Democrat" stance was an insidious political mirage: If The Third Way was anything more than an electoral strategy, why couldn't the President find any "Thirdies" to staff his White House? Indeed, after health care, even many New Democrats now believed that Bill Clinton had merely used their agenda to win office; for a time, Al From considered formally disassociating the Democratic Leadership Council from the President. "I've spent my adult life working on these ideas," a Progressive Policy Institute fellow told me over dinner one evening, with tears in his eyes, "and Bill Clinton has discredited them in two years."

The absence of prominent New Democratic advisors, apart from Al Gore, in the White House during the first few years remains something of a mystery. In a memoir of his time as a Clinton speechwriter, Michael Waldman—who came to the White House from Ralph Nader's consumer advocacy operation—admits that many of the younger members of the staff, especially those recruited by George Stephanopoulos, didn't have a clue as to what being a New Democrat meant; others, like Bob Rubin and Leon Panetta, understood only part of it—they were fiscal conservatives but traditional liberals in most other ways; still others, like Bruce Reed, were too junior to have much of an impact at first. Al From figured that Clinton was his own senior New Democratic advisor (if so, the President wasn't very successful at it during the first few years). It's more likely that Clinton—who recoiled instinctively against aides with forceful personalities or opinions—hadn't yet found a New Democrat who combined the sunniness, diffidence, and efficiency that he required in members of his inner circle; over time, Erskine Bowles, who did have those qualities, would assume that role.

———

But there was, in the Panetta era, a growing number of presidential assistants—like Waldman and Gene Sperling—who were beginning to understand, and learning to love, the nuances of the
Clinton sensibility; there also was a rivulet of actual New Democrats, like Communications Director Don Baer, who arrived
about the same time as Panetta. And Morris brought perhaps the
most influential New Democrat of the Clinton era, the pollster
Mark Penn, along with him.

In fact, Dick Morris wasn't just Dick Morris. He was a creature of his data, the ultimate poll junkie. The numbers were
crunched by the team of Penn and Doug Schoen, who had come
to prominence as pollsters for Mayor Ed Koch, a brilliant politician who successfully governed New York City (no small feat) as
a tough-on-crime moderate. In April 1995, Penn and Schoen
made their first presentation to Bill Clinton. "We had conducted a study of open-ended attitudes toward Clinton," Penn
recalled, describing a technique in which people are asked general questions: What do you like about Bill Clinton? What don't
you like? "There wasn't very much on the positive side. People
liked that he had signed the Family and Medical Leave Act"—an
extremely popular bill that had passed the Democratic Congress
during George Bush's presidency, but had never been signed by
Clinton's tone-deaf predecessor. On the negative side, people
thought Clinton was feckless, disorganized, more liberal than he
had let on during the campaign, and overmatched by the Washington establishment.

Clinton reacted positively to this bad news. Penn and Schoen
reacted positively to Clinton, who seemed to intuit the implications of everything they said. "If I hadn't gotten to know you,"

Penn later told the President, "I probably would never have voted for you." (Penn went on to poll for Al Gore in the 2000 presidential campaign. Gore fired him and hired Stan Greenberg. "I probably would have voted for Al Gore," Penn later joked, "if I hadn't gotten to know him.")

Schoen, based in New York, gradually left the Clinton account to Penn, who was a rumpled, mumbly sort, as introverted as the President was outgoing. By the end of 1995, both Penn and Morris had been integrated into the White House staff. They ran Wednesday evening "research" meetings in the White House solarium, which were religiously attended by the President and his inner circle. Penn's research was astonishing in its detail. Everything was polled. In one famous instance, Penn used data that he had already collected about what Americans liked to do on vacation to convince the President that he had chosen the wrong spot for a summer trip: Martha's Vineyard, playground of the liberal elite, was out. Wyoming—fishing and, particularly, horseback-riding (while wearing a cowboy hat)— was most definitely "in." But Penn, and even Morris, were more interested in substance than in images—even if the substance was often ridiculed as "bite-sized" and image-obsessed. Soon a welter of New Democratic ideas, shards of ideas, and bits of rhetoric that had been languishing in the midlevels of the Administration—flex-time legislation, tax relief for home sellers, school uniforms, and dozens more—were being resuscitated, as well as others that Penn limned from his constant research. Publicly, Morris said that he had a quota of two new ideas a week. Privately, he told Penn: "Never have I taken so many ideas from one person and gotten so much credit for it."

POLITICAL LEADERSHIP IS A SUBTLE art in times of plenty. When there are no great crises, there is no public demand for heroic acts. Politics becomes a parlor game, ignored by all but the most devoted citizens, a game practiced most assiduously by those interests—the business associations, trade unions, and single-issue groups—who have a direct stake in the outcome. The game turns on tactics and gestures, on the ability to placate factions, rather than to inspire the masses.

Clinton had spent most of his life dreaming of a heroic, Rooseveltian presidency, of great acts and grand gestures. But that dream ended with health care. Now he faced a more subtle challenge: In order to survive, he would have to run a tactical, defensive administration. He would have to move left and right simultaneously—left, because he needed liberal Democrats in the Congress to sustain his veto power in the face of the Republican steamroller (he also needed to protect himself from a liberal "true believer" primary challenge in 1996, which Clinton knew was a death warrant for an incumbent President). He also had to move right, to meet the more conservative mood of the American people (though he was sure it wasn't quite so conservative as the Republicans thought). Ironically, as he assessed the new playing field with Penn's and Morris's help, Clinton saw that he might also have the opportunity—if he moved carefully—to utilize a moderate bipartisan congressional majority, the coalition that had passed NAFTA, to his advantage. He was soon being ridiculed, from both ends of the political spectrum, for his new, preternatural political caution—but this was, arguably, the most astute decision-making period of his presidency. He had no credibility after the health care fiasco and the electoral rout; boldness was not a viable option. And so he moved quietly, patiently, and very, very deftly to rebuild his presidency and win reelection. It was an astonishing, if subtle, display of political virtuosity. (The carping about his unwillingness to take risks would, however, become more valid in his second term, after he had regained his popularity.)

Morris, who had no political philosophy whatever, inadvertently trivialized the bipartisan possibilities of the moment, calling it "triangulation," which fed the existing cynicism about the Third Way philosophy among already-cynical liberals and journalists. In his memoir of the Clinton years, *Behind the Oval Office*, Morris went even farther, offering a feast for cynics. At one point, he wrote, the First Lady complained about his "efforts to move to the center." As it happened, Morris's Connecticut home was being painted at the time, and he was dissatisfied with the progress of the job. "Now I used the painters as a metaphor in my reply" to the First Lady: He was the Clintons' housepainter. They summoned him every few years for cosmetic work. " 'But when you called me,' " he wrote, " 'you knew I'd want to put the furniture in the center of the room. The center, the middle,' I repeated to make sure the metaphor wasn't lost on her. 'Then I cover it up with canvas, and I paint the walls and the ceiling.' I made a painting motion with my hand. . . . 'When the walls are painted . . . I go away. Then you have four years to put the furniture back exactly as you and your husband wish.' "

Morris was, clearly, a mortal jerk. Just about everyone in the White House was appalled by him—except, perhaps, the President (who knew that the Morris–Penn route was his only way out of the morass). Most everyone outside the White House was appalled by Morris, too. "For years, the self-satisfied left has been arguing that our program was nothing more than a shallow political calculation," lamented Will Marshall, the president of the Progressive Policy Institute, who might have included the self-satisfied right in the formulation as well. "Dick Morris's career must give them great satisfaction."

In the winter of 1995, Clinton and Morris seemed a matched pair of desperate, over-the-hill political vaudevillians. The House of Representatives quickly passed most of the provisions of The Contract with America, which was Gingrich's ten-point governing doctrine, and there was a fair amount of Beltway chatter that the Speaker was now a virtual Prime Minister; certainly, he seemed the most important politician in America. (Gingrich—even more grandiose and intemperate than before and blinded by the sudden acclaim—acted as if he believed this himself. At one point, he told me that he, personally, would lead a "Wesleyan revolution" in America.) The lowest point for Clinton appeared to come on April 18, 1995, when he held a rare prime-time press conference—incredibly, only one television network chose to broadcast it—in which he was forced to say, in response to a question about his irrelevance to the policy process underway in the Republican Congress: "The President is relevant. . . . The Constitution gives me relevance; the power of our ideas gives me relevance; the record we have built up over the last two years and the things we're trying to do give me relevance."

The President would later kick himself for using that word: he had, in fact, begun to think his way through the coming battle against Gingrich—and he was not entirely pessimistic. He had taken the Speaker's measure personally, particularly in a White House meeting he and Hillary had with Gingrich and his mother after Mrs. Gingrich had publicly called the First Lady a bitch. Both Clintons found the Speaker softer than expected, and transparently "needy"—the President, who was also famously needy, but not at all soft, began to sense how Gingrich's personality might be exploited. Clinton also knew that he himself was not without weapons. He still had the veto, and enough Democrats in Congress to sustain it. He had also learned, in his first two years, that the culture of the federal capital was essentially conservative: It was far easier to oppose than to propose, the status quo was nearly as impregnable from the right as it was from the left. So he would lay low, let the Republicans try to enact the tough medicine they had promised in order to cut taxes while balancing the budget, and then he would pick them apart—especially if they actually tried to limit (to "cut," as Clinton would insist) projected increases in popular entitlement programs like Medicare. The strategy was known within the White House as "Smoke Them Out." Over time, it would work better than anyone expected.

BUT THERE WAS MORE TO the Clinton presidency than clever tactics that winter. Even in his deepest political depression, Clinton refused to succumb to expediency on issues that he considered crucial—particularly economic policy issues. In January 1995, he quickly responded to the collapse of the Mexican peso. Robert Rubin, now Treasury Secretary, told the

President that if the United States didn't create a $20 billion reserve fund for the Mexicans, there could be a financial panic and the real possibility of a global economic collapse. At a White House meeting on the afternoon of January 30, Clinton asked the new Republican leaders for help in getting a Mexican "bailout" through the Congress. "Gingrich said absolutely not," Stephanopoulos recalled. "He lectured the President about bailing out a drug-running dictatorship. He actually wanted Clinton to call Rush Limbaugh about it! It was really obnoxious."

That evening, Rubin and his deputy, Lawrence Summers, met with Clinton in the Oval Office; Stephanopoulos was there, too. Rubin had figured out a way to advance the Mexicans the money without congressional approval—but the Treasury Secretary also was concerned. A *Los Angeles Times* poll showed that the public opposed the bailout by more than a five-to-one margin. Rubin, Summers, and Stephanopoulos all remember the scene similarly: "We pointed out to him that there was no guarantee the support program would work," Rubin recalled. "And if it didn't work, it might be very damaging to his reelection prospects. But it didn't take ten minutes for him to make the decision. He just said, 'Let's do it.' "

"I was so blown away by that," Stephanopoulos recalled. "I went home that night and wrote the President a fan letter." (The Mexicans, to the surprise of almost everyone, paid back the loan ahead of schedule.)

ON THE MORNING OF April 19, 1995, the day after the press conference in which Clinton had been forced to defend his own relevance, a powerful truck bomb destroyed the Alfred P. Murrah Federal Building in Oklahoma City, killing 163 people. The explosion was the work of right-wing extremists, a Patriot's Day rejoinder to the lethal federal assault on the David Koresh cult in Waco, Texas, two years earlier. Dazed and bleeding federal employees were seen suffering on the streets of Oklahoma City; their demolished children were carried out of the ruin of the building's day care center. "I will never again use the word 'bureaucrat' publicly," Bill Clinton told Bob Rubin, in the Oval Office, a few days later. "It only plays on the resentments people feel about government."

Clinton delivered a moving eulogy at a prayer service commemorating the victims, four days after the bombing. And then, on May 5, he delivered a fighting commencement speech at Michigan State University:

> "I say this to the militias and *all others* who believe that the greatest threat to freedom comes from the government instead of from those who would take away our freedom: If you say violence is an acceptable way to make change, you are wrong. If you say government is a conspiracy to take your freedom away you are just plain wrong. . . .
>
> How dare you suggest that we in the freest nation on earth live in a tyranny? How dare you call yourselves patriots and heroes?
>
> I say to you, all of you . . . there is nothing patriotic about hating your country, or pretending that you can love your country but despise your government."

Clinton later told me that the House Republicans were as much the target of this speech as were the right-wing militias: The Gingrich movement had been built on government-bashing in the name of patriotism. The President now not only had a tactical strategy—"Smoke Them Out"—but also an intellectual rationale for his campaign against the Republican revolution, and a passion for pursuing it. After a long winter's despair, he was back, on the attack and—especially after Oklahoma City eulogy—palpably the President of the United States once more. "It was a breaking of the ice," he would say of the Michigan State speech.

The trouble was, however, Clinton didn't feel very comfortable with the "Smoke Them Out" strategy after the Republicans presented their version of a balanced budget, which included, as expected, significant bites out of Medicare and Medicaid. Almost everyone on the White House staff, especially the congressional liberals like Stephanopoulos and Panetta, still believed that presidential passivity was the best tactic. Clinton agreed that the best *politics* would be to do unto the Republicans in 1995 what they had done to him on health care in 1994: Let them suffocate under the weight of their own proposal. But the President was spiritually—and politically—uneasy with that course; he began sending signals, trying to wriggle out of it. In late May, in an interview with New Hampshire public radio, he said that he might well propose his own version of a balanced budget. This touched off a rowdy staff session in the Roosevelt Room, in which various aides argued over whether the President had or hadn't meant what he'd just said. Finally, Erskine Bowles stood up and said, "For God's sake, I'm gonna just go in and ask him."

A few minutes later, Bowles returned from the Oval Office and said yes, the President did indeed mean what he had said. Stephanopoulos, who had been enjoying the Republican agony immensely, was afraid that Dick Morris was manipulating Clinton into a grand deal that would, in the end, save Gingrich and elect Dole. After the Roosevelt Room meeting, he and Gene Sperling met with the President and tried to argue against the decision, to persuade him to wait. "Well, that's just great," Clinton exploded. "I'll just wait. I'll tear up their plan and when people say, 'Well, where's your plan?' I'll say, 'Who am I to have a plan? I'm just the President of United States.' No, I'm not going to be the way *they* were on health care."

Stephanopoulos was stunned, but acquiescent: "This is fine," he told Sperling later. "Until he blew up in there, I didn't know how gut level this was for him." In fact, it was months before Sperling realized the full implications of Clinton's decision. Stephanopoulos and Panetta had been fundamentally wrong: They had been asking Clinton to pursue a reactive, legislative-style strategy, not a presidential one. With his own balanced-budget proposal in place that autumn, Clinton was free to attack the Republicans much harder, and more confidently than he would have if he'd followed his staff's advice.

This would prove a significant turning point in the history of the Clinton presidency: the first sign that he had figured out Washington's legislative process, the beginnings of what would become a total mastery of the Republicans in the year-end budget negotiations. And it was in those negotiations—quietly, by dribs and drabs, with remarkable persistence over the years—that Clinton would get many of his most important programs enacted.

"It was a crucial moment for the Republicans, too," Stephanopoulos later recalled. "Just as we might have gotten universal health care if we had signed on to the Chafee plan, the Republicans might have won the 1996 election—they might have been able to beat Bill Clinton—if they had signed on to our balanced budget plan."

But the Gingrich Republicans—who had somehow, hilariously, borrowed both the extreme rhetoric and myopic self-righteousness of the left-wing sixties radicals whose excesses they'd promised to rectify—proved perfect opponents for the President. They refused to compromise on the budget. The new fiscal year began without an agreement, and the federal government, consequently, shut down for lack of funds in October; then, after an interim measure allowed another round of negotiations, it shut down for a second time in December. The President, of course, was complicit in this, but the Republicans, who had flaunted their intransigence throughout the year, were blamed for the spectacle. A single image sealed the deal and, in effect, ended Newt Gingrich's political career: After riding home in Air Force One from the funeral of Yitzhak Rabin that autumn, he complained to the press that he'd been given a seat in the back of the plane and hadn't had a chance to speak with Clinton. Gingrich, who was promptly caricatured as a cry-baby on the front page of the *New York Daily News*, had traveled a long way in ten months—from de facto Prime Minister to steerage.

An intriguing question about the government shutdown lingers, on both sides: Were the Republicans acting merely out of ideological rigidity and tactical idiocy, or had they been quietly assured, by Dick Morris, that if they held firm, Clinton would cave? Bob Dole, who was part of the negotiations but not privy to the various Morris scenarios, said—with ill-concealed disgust: "Lott mentioned to me a couple of times that Morris had made suggestions. If we did A or if we did B, it might work. I don't remember any of them working, though."

Indeed, Dole was in a terrible bind that autumn. He was planning to run for President in 1996, and he quickly sensed that the Republicans were going to be blamed for the budget impasse. "Maybe we made a mistake," he said years later, uncomfortable, as ever, with the first-person pronoun. "Maybe we should have taken those House guys on. . . . Somebody should have blown the whistle—if you've got the power, you have to provide the leadership. . . . But I always had the feeling that Armey's role in those meetings was to keep an eye on Bob Dole," he said, referring to House Majority Leader Richard Armey. "You know, it was 'Dole will make a deal. Dole will make a deal.' "

Dole was afraid, however, that if he did make a deal, he would empower a successful conservative challenge to his presidential candidacy, and so he kept quiet, agonizingly quiet, through what must have seemed, for an acerbic Midwestern World War II veteran, Baby Boom political hell: "Sat there for hours and hours listening to them," he said, rolling his eyes. "Newt would come up with some brilliant idea overnight—and then he'd come up with a completely different idea as we were leaving the room. This was a man with too many ideas. . . . But you had to sit through it, even though it was clear nothing was going to happen. Sat there so long, I began to get paranoid: Were they just doing this to keep me out of New Hampshire?"

Just as the House Republicans feared that Dole would make a deal, the White House staff had similar fears about the President: "You just can't put Bill Clinton alone in a room with an opponent," a top advisor with great admiration for Clinton told me. "That's not what he's good at. He'll just give away everything."

Gene Sperling was so frightened that Clinton was about to cave—that Dick Morris had cooked a secret deal—that when he heard that Leon Panetta had invited the Republicans for one last, late night negotiating session, he went to the chief of staff's office in a panic and asked, "What are we doing this for?"

"We're responsible for the United States government," Panetta said, angrily—although he, too, was worried that a significant political advantage might be squandered at the last minute. "If they want to talk, we're going to do it. Period."

At the meeting that night, Clinton not only held firm, he made a rare, face-to-face attack on an opponent. Dick Armey, a loud-mouthed Libertarian from Texas, complained that the President was trying to scare his mother-in-law about Medicare. "I don't know about your mother-in-law," Clinton hissed, "but if your budget passes, thousands of poor people are going to suffer because of your Medicaid cuts. I will never sign your Medicaid cuts. I don't care if I go down to five percent in the polls. If you want your budget passed, you're going to have to put someone else in this chair." (It should be noted that Clinton—who publicly, demagogically hammered the Republicans on Medi*care*, the very popular, if expensive, health care program for senior citizens—was far more exercised in private meetings with the Republicans about the proposed cuts in Medi*caid*, which provides health care for the poor.)

Afterward, well past midnight, the White House staff and Democratic congressional leaders gathered around the President in the Oval Office to congratulate him for standing firm. "I wish the American people could have heard what you said," the Vice President told Clinton. "I wouldn't change a single word—except maybe when you said you didn't care if your popularity got down to five percent. You could have said zero."

"Sorry, Al," Clinton said with a rueful smile. "If we hit four percent, we're caving."

CLINTON'S FORCEFULNESS on the night of the government shutdown, like his decisiveness on economic matters in general, was, literally, exceptional. Most of the time, his inability to make up his mind drove the staff crazy. "I can't tell you the number of times he called me a half hour after he had made some decision or other," said one of his chiefs of staff, "and tried to reconsider."

In part, indecision was simply the way he went about making up his mind: He was famous, among his intimates, for being able to argue an opponent's position better than the opponent did—which, inevitably, led to moments when he actually found himself believing whatever argument he was making. In fact, Clinton's decision-making process was never truly complete until he had gone all the way and actually advocated—usually briefly, always privately—the opposite position from the one he would eventually take. This was difficult for even many of those closest to him to endure. "You don't know how close he came to caving on affirmative action," George Stephanopoulos would later say.

In truth, he never came close. But, according to Hillary Clinton, he had to know exactly how "angry white males" felt—he had to feel it himself—before he could, in the summer of 1995, with an election looming (and with Dick Morris brandishing all sorts of polls showing how unpopular his position was), maintain his longtime support for affirmative action.

The decisions Clinton made on affirmative action and welfare reform, as he approached his reelection campaign of 1996, were very different and yet entirely similar. A cynic might say that he split the difference—he gave the Old Democrats affirmative action and the New Democrats welfare reform. And while his anguished equivocation undercut the moral authority of each decision, Clinton was ultimately consistent—he had stood for both throughout his political career; indeed, both were integral to his governing vision. He believed that it was fundamentally unfair to pay some people not to work while members of the "forgotten middle class" were struggling so hard to make ends meet (by the mid-nineties, two thirds of all married women were working—in most cases this was an act of economic necessity rather than of volition).

Clinton also believed that symbolic gestures of racial reconciliation—like affirmative action, which mostly benefited middle-class blacks—were not only necessary, but they also reflected an emerging American reality: It was now socially impossible to have an all-white television news team, law firm, or corporate suite (and as for affirmative action in colleges, it represented an equalizing of injustices—the children of alumni had long benefited from "legacy" admissions and students from exotic locales like . . . Arkansas had received special consideration as well). In the end, the affirmative action decision was quite personal for the President. He simply could not stand up in front of his friend Vernon Jordan or the Georgia congressman John Lewis, or his Secretary of Labor, Alexis Herman—all of whom were African-Americans who had sacrificed for the civil rights cause—and say the politically expedient words: Affirmative action is unfair and we should end it.

Welfare reform was tougher. A study by Wendell Primus, in Clinton's own Department of Health and Human Services, predicted that one million children might go without food or shelter if the plan were enacted. Most of the President's staff, including his wife, were opposed. The final version of the bill, passed by the Republicans in the Congress, had gratuitously brutal provisions—denying benefits to legal immigrants; limiting the eligibility for Medicaid and food stamps of those who didn't find work. Clinton knew that welfare policy was an inexact science; no one could predict what impact the reform would have. Any plan that eliminated the lifetime guarantee of government support to poor mothers—as he had repeatedly promised to do—was going to have inequities; a certain number of women on welfare would be incapable of working under the best of circumstances. To force them into the job market, or onto the streets, would be a cruelty beyond imagining. But if the President refused to act, after promising to "end welfare as we know it," he was sure to pay a significant political price in the coming presidential election.

At the same time, and on a more philosophical plane than pure politics, Clinton had long been convinced that outrage over the existing welfare system, particularly within the middle class, was an impediment to any sort of government activism. It was the issue that conservatives had most successfully used against liberals for a quarter century. It was the issue where the buzzwords "opportunity" and "responsibility" became real. Effective welfare reform was essential if he hoped to launch a new liberalism for the Information Age; without it, New Democrats would simply lack the credibility to propose a revised and expanded social safety net (and that was why, he admitted to me later, he should have done welfare reform before health care in 1994).

On the morning of July 31, 1996, Elaine Kamarck received an urgent call: The President wanted her to attend the final staff meeting on welfare reform. Kamarck, a New Democrat stalwart, had been part of Clinton's initial welfare task force, but she had been involved in other issues—particularly the Vice President's Reinventing Government efforts—for most of the past few years. She wondered why, at the last minute, Clinton wanted her to rejoin the internal welfare reform debate. "And then it dawned on me, when I walked into the room," she recalled. "Clinton was going to sign the bill and all these people were against it, and he needed a few more people—in addition to the Vice President and Bruce Reed—in the room to make his argument. Harold Ickes, who is a really smart pol, was the only one who got it—as soon as I walked in the room, he was just staring daggers at me."

A great many people—some surprising ones, like Bob Rubin; others, likely suspects like Donna Shalala, Panetta, and Steph-anopoulos—argued against signing the welfare reform bill that day. And Clinton, inimitably, refused to take a position . . . until he retreated to the Oval Office with Gore, Reed, Panetta, and several others. Panetta argued even more vehemently in private against signing the bill. The President asked Al Gore what he thought. "I think the system is fundamentally broken," the Vice President said. "It's worth the risk."

Clinton nodded his head and said, "I want to sign it. Let's do it."

The decision was perhaps the most controversial, for liberals, of Clinton's years in office; old friends like Peter and Marion Wright Edelman were infuriated and said so. "I always thought he would veto the bill," said Peter Edelman, who had been working on the welfare issue in the Health and Human Services Department and resigned from the Administration when Clinton signed the bill. "I was, and remain, disappointed with the President for several reasons. First, his tendency to pick on people who don't have the political power to oppose him, especially on the crime and welfare reform issues. Second, his personal behavior. And the glitz factor—all that fund-raising, the Hollywood business."

But David Ellwood, a welfare expert who left Health and Human Services and returned to Harvard University a year before Clinton signed the bill, had a more interesting, and nuanced, reaction to the ultimate welfare reform legislation. Ellwood had written a seminal book, *Poor Support*, about the perverse incentives of the existing system. But the reality of welfare reform—the idea that poor women and children might actually be forced into destitution by a purposeful government action—humbled him; he began to think it might be best to test the program in ten states, then study the results and make a more considered decision. "The President said he'd come back and fix the bad things in the bill," he told me. "But with a Republican Congress, who could be sure of that?"

And while Ellwood remained concerned about the potential long-term impacts of welfare reform, especially if there was an economic recession, he was, in the end, surprised by the success of Clinton's plan. "The results are much better than I expected," he said, fours years after the reform was passed. "And the public knows only half the story. They know that welfare rolls have been almost cut in half. The strong economy helped that—and it's also true that there were a lot of people who already held jobs in the underground economy who were receiving benefits illegally. But what people don't know is that the President did exactly what he said he was going to do: he made work pay. He did it incrementally, but the results have been dramatic. In 1986, a single mother who left welfare for work could expect to make about nineteen hundred dollars more than she was getting from the government and lose her health benefits. In 1999, she gets seven thousand dollars more and keeps her health benefits. People have responded to these incentives. There's been an enormous increase in the workforce participation rate among the poorest women: from thirty to fifty-five percent in the last three years. We've never seen anything like it."

A study, published in 2001 by Wendell Primus and Allen Dupree—the same Wendell Primus who had predicted social disaster and then quit the Clinton administration in 1995—showed another remarkable effect of welfare reform: The number of children living with single parents dropped by 8 percent in the five years after the bill passed. "Among blacks . . . marriage seems to be staging a significant comeback," noted Mickey Kaus, the journalist who had been the most passionate proselytizer for welfare reform. "The percentage of all black children raised by married parents jumped from 34.8 percent to 38.9 percent during the period [studied by Primus and Dupree], a ten percent increase in just five years."

It seemed that Clinton had not only made work pay, but he'd also removed the disincentive to marriage that had been an unintended consequence of the old welfare system, which only visited benefits upon single mothers. So there was an answer to the "culture of poverty" arguments long posed by conservatives—but it was an answer that combined conservative values ("responsibility") with liberal spending ("opportunity"). This was, perhaps, the purest demonstration of the substance and possibilities of The Third Way.

It was also a demonstration of the most admirable aspect of Bill Clinton's record in office—and the least Clintonian: a triumph of persistence, not charisma. For six years, the President worked with great discipline and patience to force a reluctant Republican Congress to spend more money on a surprising array of programs, especially those that raised the incomes of the working poor. These efforts had none of the drama of the government shutdowns or the health care debate; they were nearly invisible, in fact, hidden in the massive, incomprehensible budget "reconciliation" packages negotiated each fall. Most of the victories were tiny by federal standards, but the numbers gathered cumulative force over time—even in 1998 and 1999, with Washington allegedly paralyzed by the Lewinsky scandal and impeachment proceedings, Clinton continued his work, winning a few hundred million dollars here, a billion there for programs he favored. Head Start grew from $2.8 billion in 1993 to $6.3 billion in 2000; child care supports grew from $4.5 billion to $12.6 billion; the Earned Income Tax Credit, from $12.4 billion in 1993 to $30.5 billion in 2000; AmeriCorps, the national service program that Republicans attempted to kill from the moment Clinton proposed it, actually grew from $373 million in 1994 to $473 million in 2000. The list is comprehensive, involving almost every area of domestic spending (and, in his second term, defense appropriations as well)—and it has a New Democrat bent, a tendency to favor cash and tax credits over the establishment of new federal bureaucracies.

Indeed, in his eight years in office, Clinton only created one new bureaucracy—AmeriCorps—and that program was semi-private, and run almost entirely through the states. "He was more effective than any other President, by far, in using the budget process to get what he wanted," said Norman Ornstein, a fellow at the American Enterprise Institute who specialized in congressional affairs. "Of course, the Republicans—who were totally inept—gave him a lot of help."

The government shutdowns had neutered the Republicans in the annual negotiations with the President, robbing them of their most potent threat; but Clinton still had the veto, and the ability to delay the process and raise the prospect of yet another government shutdown (for which the Republicans now knew they'd be blamed). He could turn each autumn into anguish, especially in the even-numbered years, when the members of Congress were desperate to return home to campaign for reelection. "You have to give him a lot of credit for adapting his strategy to the new realities after the Republicans took control," Ornstein said. "He had an incredible feedback mechanism—if something didn't work, he tried something else. He would retreat, delay, come back with another proposal—get a half of what he wanted, a quarter, an eighth. But he'd almost always get something."

BY THE BEGINNING OF THE 1996 presidential campaign, only a year after the Republicans had taken control of the Congress, Clinton was once again the most formidable politician in the country. His reelection campaign was astonishingly easy; it was probably decided by the time he pronounced, in his State of the Union address, that "the era of big government is over." The hapless Republican candidates for President proceeded to cut each other up in Iowa and New Hampshire; Steve Forbes and Pat Buchanan completed the demolition of Bob Dole long before the general election campaign began—although, in truth, Dole had always been a far more effective politician in private, in the closed-committee negotiations on Capitol Hill, than in public; by 1996, he simply seemed too old to be President.

As Clinton's inevitability settled in on the astonished Republicans, so did another reality: Their Congress would have to modify its image, and get some things accomplished, if they didn't want to lose what they had gained in 1994. And so, as the year progressed, the Gingrich Revolution found itself passing not just welfare reform (with significant funding for the sorts of support programs—like day care—that David Ellwood thought would never pass a Republican Congress), but also an increase in the minimum wage and the Kennedy–Kassebaum health care bill, which guaranteed the extension of insurance to workers who lost, or left, their jobs. "They were making all these deals with Clinton," said Bob Dole, who resigned from the Senate to pursue his campaign and was hoping to campaign against gridlock. "And I'm thinking, 'Guys! Don't pass anything else! Don't throw me over!' "

IN THE SUMMER OF 1996, the President asked Erskine Bowles, Mickey Kantor, and Vernon Jordan to start thinking about an agenda for his second term. The blueprint they produced was a management consultant's dream: orderly, comprehensive, worthy and, in some ways, ambitious. But there was no magic in it. Clinton's grand first-term dreams had shriveled into a set of proposals; the President, convinced of the futility of trying to impose inspiration upon an apathetic public, had redacted himself. He was no longer a romantic visionary, but a mechanic now, brilliant at the filigree work—but less, somehow, than the fresh breeze promised in 1992.

He would spend all of 1997 working on a balanced-budget agreement with the Republicans. The media would spend most of 1997 thrashing their way through another semi-scandal: the outrageous efforts by Clinton and Gore to raise a ton of money for their reelection campaigns. Again, a hilarious cast of smarmy characters would be unearthed—Johnny Chung, Charlie Trie, the Riady family of Indonesia—and, again, Clinton would rub very close to the edge of legality and well past the borders of propriety (allowing major campaign contributors to buy access to the President and, in several cases, overnight stays in the Lincoln Bedroom). There would be the appearance of serious offenses, particularly in the area of Chinese high-tech and military espionage; but, on closer inspection, the breaches of security evaporated into the nuanced fog of business transacted in a global economy.

In the process, the Balanced Budget Agreement that the President was able to negotiate with the Republicans—the first nominally balanced budget in thirty years—received insufficient attention. It was, in a way, the ultimate demonstration of the New Clintonism. The real victory wasn't in the "zero" at the bottom line, but in the dozens of line-item skirmishes won. Indeed, Clinton managed to gain approval for several new, and rather large, social programs that had been at the heart of his own wish list from the moment he had announced his intention to run for President. There was more than $30 billion in new tax credits for higher education; in effect, this made the first two years of college a middle class entitlement (by 1999, an astonishing ten million of the fourteen million Americans eligible would take advantage of this credit). There was also $24 billion for a children's health program that would, theoretically, provide insurance to every child whose parents could not afford it—the beginning, the President hoped, of an incremental effort to provide access to health insurance to those most in need of it. He also was able to make the welfare reform revisions he had promised, restoring support to legal immigrants and increasing the funds in a variety of programs targeted to help single mothers joining the work force. Gene Sperling estimates that the 1997 budget deal provided $70 billion, over five years, to families with incomes of less than $30,000.

This was an achievement ignored by Clinton's critics on the left (who wanted bigger social programs), on the right (who wanted less spending), in the press (who mostly didn't notice), and in academia. "These aren't big pieces of legislation. These are scraps off the table," said Stephen Hess, of the Brookings Institution. "It ain't the GI Bill of Rights. It's not Social Security. It's not a vision, it's ad hockery. I'm not sure how different this presidency is going to look than Calvin Coolidge's."

But the college tax credit plan passed in 1997 was *larger* than the GI Bill of Rights, which only applied to returning World War II veterans; and there was an almost poignant stubbornness in Clinton's efforts to slowly reconstruct universal health insurance and to fight the Republicans, line by line, through the budget each year. The quiet seriousness of this effort was the precise opposite of the President's feckless public image. In fact, Bill Clinton—who had the unfortunate habit of describing character as a "journey, not a destination"—had demonstrated, over time, that persistence was his strongest character trait. In this case, it was persistence of the most high-minded sort—in the service of his political beliefs, not his ambition—and the result was perhaps the most important substantive achievement of his presidency: a government that had dramatically improved the lives of millions of the poorest, hardest-working Americans.

But there was a political price to be paid for incrementalism—for Newt Gingrich and Bill Clinton both. Gingrich soon faced a Jacobin revolution from below in which most of his top lieutenants were implicated. Clinton faced a more existential dilemma: Incrementalism was too subtle a story for the all-news cable networks and the front pages. There was a news vacuum that needed to be filled. In 1998, it would be.

CHAPTER
SEVEN

"You just know he's pulling an all-nighter," Mandy Grunwald said on the evening before Bill Clinton admitted to a grand jury that his denials of sexual contact with Monica Lewinsky had been, to use his term of art, "legally accurate" but "incomplete." Grunwald, who had been cut loose by the President—along with the pollster Stan Greenberg—after the election catastrophe of 1994, laughed wistfully and began to reminisce about all-nighters past. (She remained loyal to the Clintons throughout, though, and would return as media consultant to Hillary's successful 2000 Senate campaign.)

To Clinton's circle of friends and employees, his habits, excesses, and eccentricities had become both legendary and entirely predictable over the years. The Lewinsky affair was shocking and disgraceful but not unpredictable. The reactions of the press, the Republicans, and the public had gone pretty much as expected (the press and the Republicans were a lot more upset than the public seemed to be). That the President would some-how survive the squalid moment seemed likely, too. He always did. But there would be a difference this time. In the past— when the Gennifer Flowers and draft controversies had blown up during the 1992 campaign and Clinton had somehow sur-vived, when Whitewater had been endured, when Gingrich had taken over the Congress and Clinton had outwitted him—there had always been a certain exhilaration inherent in watching the President elude the posse. Early on, James Carville had asked Clinton about his tendency to live dangerously.

"Well, they haven't caught me yet," Clinton replied.

But now, he'd been caught. He would survive yet again—and even thrive, for a time—but he had damaged himself irrevoca-bly. His behavior, during the affair and after, was both outra-geous and pathetic. He had lawyered his way through an act of passion, redefining what "sex" was and what "is" is; he had be-trayed his wife and staff and given a sword to those who hated what he'd stood for; he'd wasted eight months in a lie. He would survive—thanks in part, and yet again, to the incompetent vehe-mence of his opponents—but there would be no joy in watching him elude the posse this time. Just embarrassment and disgust.

IN THE BEGINNING, it had seemed remarkable—and charming, in an accessible, collegiate sort of way—that a man who stood a reasonable chance of becoming President of the United States would pull all-nighters with the gang whenever he was tested, and often when he was not. Most campaign metaphors are martial and someone had nicknamed the strategic nexus of the Clinton Little Rock headquarters the War Room. But the reality was more generationally appropriate: the War Room was actually the Dorm Room—a floating bull session, sticky with spilled Diet Coke, reeking of stale pepperoni with extra cheese. There was a precocious fizz to it, which extended to the candidate himself. Often, the all-nighters were about policy or philosophy. Clinton loved to talk about serious things. "I keep thinking of the conversations we had, the sense of possibility," an old friend of the Clintons lamented in the midst of the Lewinsky denouement. "It's completely gone now—thrown away. I can't tell you how painful that is."

But even in the beginning, there was a strangeness to Clinton's endless chatter. There was an odd, vacant, needy quality to it: It was the conversational equivalent of someone standing too close to you (although there was never any real intimacy to it). This was especially true late at night: He would go on and on. He would pick up speed and intensity as the hours stretched, like an eighteen-wheeler careening along the interstate after midnight. Nothing much was ever accomplished in a Clinton all-nighter. The sessions tended to be retrospective, not prospective. Clinton would chew over the events of the day and revisit decisions he'd already made rather than plan his next steps.

The all-nighters waned after he became President, but not quickly enough. In 1993, Clinton's rambling policy seminars on Bosnia—they were the daytime equivalent of all-nighters—startled crisp, military sorts like Colin Powell. But gradually the President did become more disciplined. The new style was set by Clinton's ultrabrisk, ultracorporate chief of staff in the second term, the North Carolina businessman Erskine Bowles, who had actually made a first-term efficiency study of the President's propensity for wasting time. By the second term, the all-nighter era was long past. "I don't think," a Clinton veteran mused, "there's anybody left around here he likes enough to stay up with all night."

Still, moments of personal crisis, especially those related to Clinton's seething anger over Kenneth Starr's metastasizing Whitewater investigation, could send the President hurtling back to the dorm. "That man is evil," he would tell friends. "When this thing is over, there's only going to be one of us left standing. And it's going to be me."

The public, which came to know far too much about Bill Clinton, never got to see that angry, adolescent side of him. The public never saw the temper tantrums, the almost hilarious self-involvement, the sense of personal entitlement that led him to indulge his appetites with a White House intern. They never saw the childishness. "I'm so angry at you," the President once told a political ally, "I'm not going to talk to you today."

The public never saw all this because Bill Clinton was protected by the most sophisticated communications apparatus in the history of American politics. There were the weekly Penn meetings in the solarium, which continued even after the 1996 campaign had ended—and there was an equally sophisticated, fabulously lethal, rapid-response media operation that stood prepared to defend the President against any form of attack. Over time, the Dorm Room really had become a War Room. If the Republicans had broken new ground in the art of political attack in the eighties, Clinton had perfected the instant counterattack in the nineties—it was, in fact, a necessary means of survival in the partisan Armageddon of the Gingrich era. A phalanx of zeal-ous Clinton defenders was on call to slash or smear the opposi-tion, to answer charges, and knock down unfavorable stories (sometimes before they appeared). The Oppo team performed both publicly and surreptitiously. James Carville, the fiercest and most highly skilled of the President's hammers, actually wrote a book entitled *We're Right, They're Wrong*. No quarter was given. The decibel level was ludicrous. Most normal people—under-standing that there was very little at stake in a time of unprece-dented peace and prosperity—tuned out, but the threat of a thermonuclear reaction from the White House often proved a useful, if not always successful, deterrent to some of those think-ing about joining the swarm of Clinton assailants.

To be fair, the President wasn't as vicious or petty a combatant as his Republican opponents. Not at the start, at least. But, as the Clintons' policy goals were foiled—especially after the 1994 bloodbath—and the personal campaign against the President and First Lady escalated, both Clintons came to see the opposi-tion as deranged, unscrupulous, and organized. And it was true that the Clintons were afflicted by a steady barrage from bottom-feeding tabloid profiteers, by an almost laughably unsa-vory catalogue of right-wing ideologues, and by an impossibly pompous press. The Starr investigation—which never did find *any* evidence of criminal misuse of office by Bill Clinton, either as President or as governor of Arkansas—was a constant, infuri-ating presence in their lives. It seems probable that the passion of Clinton's Lewinsky denials was intensified by his outrage that his enemies had finally found a pretext to penetrate his personal life.

The Natural

In a way, the most startling aspect of Clinton's Lewinsky capitulation, in late August 1998, was seeing the President suddenly all alone, his communications apparatus useless—spin-less for once. This was probably unavoidable. The political team was kept in the dark by the President's lawyers, who were having a difficult time getting Clinton to do the right thing. Uninformed, the President's Oppo gang was momentarily silenced. A shattering silence it was.

IN WASHINGTON, NEWS IS a parlor game. Newspaper stories, especially those in the elite press, come encrypted with secret messages. Sometimes the messages are very personal. The lead article in the *New York Times* on Friday, August 14, 1998, three days before Clinton was to testify before the grand jury, was just such a story. The headline was stunning: "President Weighs Admitting He Had Sexual Contacts." The source of the story, it was widely assumed by other Clinton advisors, was the President's old friend and legal advisor Mickey Kantor. The media's first impression was that this was business as usual, the beginning of a new spin cycle—that it was a controlled leak, with the White House taking charge of the Lewinsky story and preparing the public for what was about to happen, so that the president's "revised" testimony wouldn't come as a complete shock. But there was much more to it than that; indeed, the story was part of an entirely bizarre melodrama taking place within the White House. Someone close to the President was "sending a message," a longtime friend of the Clintons told me, and the message was: Stop dawdling, Mr. President. Face the facts. Tell your wife and staff that you are about to change your story.

The *Times* account shocked a great many people close to the President. Clinton's press secretary, Mike McCurry, said he had no idea it was coming. Rahm Emanuel, the advisor who had taken George Stephanopoulos's cubicle adjacent to the Oval Office, said he didn't know about it, either. Apparently, the story also surprised the First Lady.

How on earth was *that* possible?

Of course, by August 14, Mrs. Clinton had to know the same things the rest of the world knew. By then, Monica Lewinsky had decided to cooperate with the prosecution; by then, the rumors of a stained dress—a piece of evidence that originally had seemed too tawdry to be real—had been confirmed. Also, on August 13, as reported in *The Breach* by Peter Baker of the *Washington Post*, Clinton had dispatched his lawyer, David Kendall, to tell the First Lady that . . . well, one wonders just exactly what Kendall *told* Mrs. Clinton and how he said it, and how she reacted. So it is entirely possible, if quite incredible, that the President had not yet sat down with his wife and actually confessed. (He'd never been very good at delivering bad news.) If so, the First Lady must have been infuriated by the silence, for reasons both personal and political. Clinton had been as adamant, and perhaps more effective, in his private denials of the affair as he had been in public. He'd work his signature magic, stare his interlocutors in the eye, drape an arm over their shoulders, and then, deeply, mournfully, he'd say, "If you only knew the truth."

At one point early on, Mrs. Clinton had asked him point-blank, "So who *is* this Monica Lewinsky?" The President's response apparently had been legally accurate . . . but incomplete. One imagines the First Lady torturing the President with her silence—a far more effective tactic than blowing up at him—in mid-August, waiting for him to come clean. But, again, no one really knows what was going on between them.

Obviously, there had been a devastating personal betrayal. But the First Lady believed she had been betrayed politically as well. Clinton had handed their mortal enemy, Kenneth Starr, the power to destroy all that they'd worked for. And there was probably some anger, too, that the President had worked out the strategy for handling this most important crisis—and was about to change his testimony—without her.

In the days that followed, there was speculation in the press that the family trauma—the cool body language, the summoning of Jesse Jackson to the family quarters, the sheer embarrassment—was something of a ruse, an effort to make the First Lady seem less culpable after she had defended her husband so vehemently (and spun out conspiracy theories so ardently) on *Today* in January. But many of those close to the Clintons believed that the First Lady had actually bought her husband's story. "She thought his messing around was over," a friend said. "She assumed that living in the White House was like being in jail."

On Saturday, August 15, the day after the *New York Times* story, Bob Woodward wrote, in the *Washington Post*, that "a person who has spoken to the president's legal team" had said on Friday that Clinton had "not prepared the family," and "he has got a lot of work to do with the family."

At some point during the course of that weekend, presumably, Bill Clinton did sit down with Hillary Clinton and told her what he would tell the grand jury on Monday. (It will be interesting to see if either of the Clintons chooses to describe that moment in their respective memoirs.)

THE PLAN WAS THAT THE President would speak to the nation on the evening of August 17, after he'd testified to the grand jury, and apologize for what he had done. He did speak, and he did apologize, sort of. But it was a grudging apology. In fact, the real emotion in the speech wasn't contrition, but an assault on Starr. Clinton explained that he had "misled" the public because of personal embarrassment, out of concern for his family, but also because:

"The independent counsel moved on [from the Whitewater investigation] to my staff and friends. Then into my private life. And the investigation itself is under investigation. This has gone on too long, cost too much, and hurt too many innocent people . . .

"Even presidents have private lives. It is time to stop the pursuit of personal destruction and the prying into private lives and get on with our national life."

The sentiments were worthy—but, as always with Clinton, the body language was far more important than the words: His tone was angry, unapologetic, ungracious. It was, perhaps, his least effective public moment in the White House—and the most embarrassing four minutes that an American President had suffered through since Richard Nixon's maudlin resignation speech. But it was nothing compared to the embarrassments to come.

It is possible, indeed probable, that nothing Clinton could have said that night would have staunched the insanity of the next six months—the release of Starr's gratuitously prurient "report" of the details of the Lewinsky affair, the televising of Clinton's grand jury testimony, the Republicans' futile and nihilistic impeachment of the President. But there were those who believed that a more heartfelt, emotional Clinton apology on August 17 would have rallied public opinion and further isolated Starr, forcing a more circumspect Starr Report and causing the Republicans to think twice about impeachment. The cool, defiant nature of the speech was certainly out of character for this most emotionally astute of presidents—and this was largely attributable to the fact that Clinton's communication machine had, for once, broken down.

Just before the President went on the air at 9 P.M., in the same White House Map Room where he had been questioned by Starr, Tim Russert, NBC's Washington bureau chief, reported that he had spoken with White House aides who said the purpose of the speech would be "candor, contrition, and, they hope, closure." He said the President was going to offer a fulsome apology to the nation, that he would be a "good cop" and not attack the independent counsel—the dirty work would be left to his staff. "The President will take a big step," Russert said, "but it will not be the end of this."

Russert had been misled by his White House sources. Aides—particularly Paul Begala and Rahm Emanuel, who had written a more contrite and less combative draft—had obviously been engaged in wishful thinking. They had briefed the press for the speech they *hoped* Clinton would deliver. That briefing constituted an astounding breach of "message discipline" at a crucial moment.

Another important advisor who may have chosen the moment to pursue a personal agenda was the First Lady. "It's your speech, say what you want," the First Lady was reported to have said—and most commentators took this to be a form of encouragement, that Hillary Clinton had wanted her husband to deliver a defiant, avenging message. A second popular theory was that this was the speech that the president *thought* his wife wanted him to deliver. But the truth of the matter was far more brutal.

Under normal circumstances, Mrs. Clinton's role would have been to calm her husband, saying, "You're too angry—stop yourself," when he came out "seething" from his grand jury testimony. But she rather pointedly chose not to do that. When she said "It's your speech, do what you want," during a last-minute, prespeech strategy session in the solarium, she was really telling the President, "I don't want to have any part of this."

And so, for once, the President stood before the country without staff or spouse to tamp down his wilder impulses. It wasn't pretty. But the results would have probably been just as grisly if the President had had the benefit of his usual spin team. He might have seemed less angry, more contrite, but he would still have been stuck with his untenable verbal fudgery: that his previous denial of a sexual relationship with Lewinsky, delivered under oath in the Paula Jones sexual harassment case, had been "legally accurate." In other words, Bill Clinton had decided to acknowledge the most hilariously absurd and mingy rumor that had been floated during the eight months of Lewinskyiana: that he believed oral sex was not sex.

The only possible response of a loyal Clintonite to such a remarkable proposition was silence, and pained silence was the most favorable reaction that the President received as the reality of his statement was absorbed during the next forty-eight hours. Privately, the White House staff was aghast. More than a few of his closest advisors—especially those who had vehemently defended the President on television during the past eight months—felt personally betrayed. There was some disingenuousness in that: Within the Clinton inner circle, the long-standing assumption about Monica Lewinsky had been the same as the general assumptions about Paula Jones and Gennifer Flowers and, more recently, Katherine Willey, who claimed that Clinton had groped her in the Oval Office—that the President had undoubtedly glanced their way, and had perhaps done a bit more than glance, but the actual facts probably didn't bear much resemblance to the stories the women were telling.

In this case, though, they had. The reality of the Lewinsky affair was astonishing in its selfishness, crudeness, and banality. It had happened in the White House. With an intern. It involved acts—and the President had now admitted as much—more exploitative than romantic. Dee Dee Myers, Clinton's first-term press secretary, was not merely upset that the President hadn't told the truth. "I never believed," she wrote in *Time*, "that Bill Clinton would actually risk his presidency—a job he had studied, dreamed about, and prepared for since he was a kid—for something so frivolous, so reckless, so small."

This was an expurgated version of what some of Clinton's oldest friends were saying privately. "I'm mad as hell," a former high-ranking administration official told me the day after the President's speech. "Here you had the most tactical, risk-averse President we've ever had—all that polling and market-testing before he'd even propose the tiniest of Dick Morris's 'bite-sized' social programs. And at the same time, for reasons that are inexplicable to me, he takes these huge, absurd personal risks and throws it all away. You know, you hear the same comment over and over from working people, 'He's an asshole.' Well, I'm with them."

On the day after Clinton's appearance, Starr called Dick Morris to testify before the grand jury. It was brilliant choreography. Afterward, Morris announced to the press that Clinton had consulted him in January, after the Lewinsky story broke, and had asked him to poll the possibility of an apology. Morris claimed to have found that the public would tolerate a confession of adultery, but not an admission that he'd lied in his Paula Jones deposition. This nauseating revelation, which was almost lost in the torrent of news, seemed to encapsulate all the worst aspects of the Clinton administration: The President was a man who would actually poll whether or not he should tell the truth. (In his book *A Vast Conspiracy*, Jeffrey Toobin later revealed that Mark Penn had been testing possible language for Clinton's apology speech.)

Within days, various staff members—and the President himself, who knew that he'd screwed up—began to think about taking another run at an apology, in an interview, perhaps, or in response to a question at a press conference. "He can still finish the conversation," one aide said. And he tried. And tried. In interviews, in speeches, at prayer breakfasts. He apologized to the Lewinsky family, to his family, to the members of his Cabinet, to the Democratic Party, to the American people. At times, he did so with tears in his eyes.

MEANWHILE, THE PRESIDENT was at work on another, far more questionable, strategy to turn the nation's attention away from the Lewinsky scandal. For nearly two weeks before Clinton's grand jury date, the Administration had been planning an assault on the guerrilla infrastructure of Osama bin Laden, the Saudi millionaire who, according to the White House, had masterminded the bombings, on August 7, 1998, of United States embassies in Kenya and Tanzania. Early on the morning of August 20, three days after his testimony, Clinton approved a cruise-missile attack on a pharmaceuticals factory in Sudan and on a guerrilla camp in Afghanistan, both of which were said to have been linked to bin Laden.

The attacks were ineffective, to say the least—and a rather suspicious use of presidential power besides. It remains an open question whether the pharmaceuticals factory had any link at all to bin Laden, and sending cruise missiles against a desert camp was the most oafish sort of overkill. Indeed, these attacks had a distressing similarity to the plot of the movie *Wag the Dog*, which had opened—uncannily—about the same time as the Lewinsky scandal did. In the film, political consultants concoct an imaginary war in Albania to distract attention from a presidential sex scandal involving a young "Firefly Girl." And there were suspicions, even among the President's own foreign policy team, that the scandal had influenced Clinton's decision to go after bin Laden: "This is a man who has always had a very difficult time making up his mind about taking military action," said a ranking foreign policy expert. "This time, he was very decisive. I believe it was the right thing to do, but you can't tell me it was unrelated to the domestic political situation."

The funny thing was, it sort of worked. Pentagon officials suddenly were stealing airtime from prosecutors on the evening news. The overwhelming, and rather surreal, assessment was that the President had done the right thing. The public supported the bombings. And so did many Republicans. Moreover, Clinton's decisiveness gave pause to those who had been saying that his presidency was crippled, unable to function, lacked the "moral authority" to act in a crisis. Senator Orrin Hatch, Republican of Utah, who had called the president a "jerk" after the Monday night speech, quickly "applauded" the President's actions and hoped that more would follow.

AND SO BEGAN THE MOST lurid month in the history of the American presidency, a month punctuated by the release of the Starr Report and the televising of Clinton's grand jury testimony in mid-September, a deranged time when even the most level-headed members of the political and journalistic communities seemed to come unhinged. In the midst of the mayhem, the internet magazine *Salon* released a story that the rest of the press—in an inexplicable spasm of responsible behavior—had passed on: Congressman Henry Hyde of Illinois, the

Republican chairman of the Judiciary Committee, who was to preside over the impeachment hearings, had had an adulterous liaison forty years earlier. "Ugly times call for ugly tactics," *Salon's* editor explained, creating an instant epitaph for an era.

For a time, the President seemed to be in desperate trouble. The word spread—and no one was quite sure how it spread—that his grand jury testimony was an embarrassment: He had been successfully cornered, lost his temper, stumbled, seemed foolish. Democrats grew nervous, even moderate Democrats. A few days before Clinton's testimony was broadcast, Representative Jim Moran of Virginia, who was one of the President's closest allies in Congress, told CNN: "There is some hemorrhaging going on within the Democratic party. . . . The President has to come up with a way, in my opinion, to stop this." What sort of way? "I'm just not creative enough to think of a way other than resignation," Moran said. "But maybe he can."

And then, on Monday, September 21, the scandal reached its apogee. A nation gathered around its television sets expecting to see the President of the United States make a fool of himself, turn purple, scream like a banshee, and storm out of the room.

But Bill Clinton didn't turn purple. On my television, he seemed sort of salmon pink, with several shiny patches of sweat on his forehead; aside from that, he was the same Bill Clinton we'd always seen in public—which is to say, charming, mesmerizing, and wicked smart. A bit too smart, at times. The testimony contained one of the monumental Clinton howlers: "Well, it depends on what your definition of 'is' is." It also contained one of the more improbable arguments in the history of human sexuality—that oral sex isn't really sex. But apart from those moments, Clinton did about as well as could be expected under the circumstances. He was at once gallant and brutal about Lewinsky; he was credibly remorseful about his actions; he was appropriately indignant about the motives of the prosecutorial army that had been pursuing him; his decision not to discuss sexual details seemed eminently rational. Indeed, the testimony proved to be a rare and unexpected event: It was subtle, complicated, enigmatic, slow-moving—by its very pace, it defied the prevailing hyperbole and tamped down the scandal.

When it was over, the fever had broken. The cable-news hysteria subsided. There was a new, oddly subdued air to the endless commentary. And even the Republicans seemed taken aback. How on earth had Clinton survived *that*? At the White House press briefing, a few hours after the tape had been aired, Mike McCurry was asked: "Can the President use something like this"—the taped testimony—"to turn it around and perhaps pull in some support?"

McCurry smiled. "I don't know how you use a day like this to rally support," he said.

By the time *Larry King Live* rolled around that night, with a special two-hour extravaganza, the mood shift was palpable. Most of the guests thought the President had had a "good day." The White House seemed revitalized, and its spin operation was back in gear. The President's speechwriter, Paul Begala, who had gone to ground in disgust and anger over Clinton's behavior, suddenly reemerged as Larry King's guest—a chirpy presidential cheerleader once more. "Is this something that we impeach a president over?" he asked, adding that the prosecutors had been fundamentally unfair: "There were eighty-some-odd questions about sex and zero about Whitewater."

At the beginning of the Clinton administration, Begala had invented a new, acronymic term of opprobrium—BAU, meaning Business As Usual. BAU was originally a bad thing; the Clinton administration was anti-BAU, they were going to be fundamentally, radically different from the Republican fuddy-duddies who'd gone before. Now Begala was celebrating, with no small relief, a return to BAU, Clinton style—blithely spinning, attacking Starr, and seeming very pleased with himself.

THE PUBLIC LOVED THE LEWINSKY show, for a time. The ratings of the all-news networks soared. Newspapers and magazines did well, too. The vast popularity of the soap opera was, in a way, a precursor of "reality" shows like *Survivor*, which would suddenly, and perhaps not coincidentally, become hot just as Clinton was leaving office. But the ratings only held for the prurient stage of the drama; the story was, in effect, over after Clinton's testimony was aired. The distended impeachment hearings were judged wasteful and unnecessary by the folks— the worst sort of television, a foregone conclusion.

And when it all had been digested, public opinion had shifted not a whit. The President's job approval ratings remained very high, in the 60 percent range—he would leave office with the highest sustained job approval ratings of any President since John F. Kennedy. His personal approval ratings were lower, of course. It was difficult to imagine any civilian answering in the affirmative if asked, "Do you approve of the President's personal behavior?" Of course, many secret sympathies were undoubtedly harbored, especially among those Clinton's age, who had navigated themselves—shakily—through the uncertain moral shoals of the late twentieth century. Americans have a quiet appreciation of rogues, and a sophisticated ability to distinguish rogues from scoundrels, and Clinton had been judged the former.

Even in the white heat of the scandal, in the days after his grand jury testimony, overwhelming numbers—two thirds, according to most polls—opposed impeachment; a solid majority favored an alternate punishment option: censure by Congress (a legislative slap on the wrist). When asked how they'd vote if the 1996 election were to be held again, the results were almost exactly the same as they'd been: 46 percent said Clinton, 36 percent said Dole, 11 percent said Perot. It was as if the name "Lewinsky" had never been heard in the land.

Although, not quite so: The Republicans suffered, grievously. They lost five seats in the congressional elections that fall, which was very rare for a midterm election during a President's sixth year in office. Newt Gingrich suffered an appropriately Jacobin fate, becoming a target of his own hotheads. He resigned as Speaker after the elections, left the House of Representatives, and soon left his second wife, Marianne, and married a young woman with whom he'd been having an extramarital affair. His reign had lasted exactly four—entirely disastrous—years. Gingrich's successor, Robert Livingston of Louisiana, also resigned after rumors spread that he, too, had experienced moments of untoward humanity with women not his wife in the past.

The press suffered more subtly, but no less profoundly, than the Republicans did. A Harris Poll showed that journalists were now held in the lowest public esteem of any professional group, lower even than lawyers.

This mystified Washington. William Bennett, the former Reagan Education Secretary who had built a cottage industry out of books that compiled stories about "virtues" (he was also the younger brother of the President's lawyer, Robert Bennett), now hustled forth with a new book called *The Death of Outrage*, and made a national tour lamenting the moral insensitivity of the American people. The editorial pages of both the *New York Times* and *Washington Post* had sounded, in the midst of the scandal, every bit as intemperate as the editorial page of *The Wall Street Journal.* Just before the testimony was broadcast, the *Washington Post* had proposed that "invoking the majesty of the impeachment clause against behavior such as this is somehow to cheapen the clause"—in other words, the President lacked the stature to be impeached. This had become the conventional wisdom among the Washington Establishment: Why didn't he have the class to resign?

It was nearly impossible to find a political commentator who had anything measured to say about Bill Clinton. Even the normally understated dean of political columnists, the *Washington Post*'s David Broder, had mournfully concluded: "Like Nixon, he has done things of importance for the country, but in every important way, he has diminished the stature and reduced the authority of the Presidency. He may hold on, but when he said of the investigation of his activities, 'This has gone on too long,' the words could equally apply to his own tenure."

HOW, THEN, TO EXPLAIN THE contrast between the intensity of outrage in Washington and the laissez-faire attitude toward the President's immorality among the citizens of the most religious of Western democracies? It seemed an unprecedented disparity, and quite fascinating. It was especially entertaining to watch the commentariat—which had been predicting for months that the public would soon share its anti-Clinton obsession—try to explain why that hadn't happened. But then, the public reaction defied illogic. Americans had judged the Lewinsky affair a delicious, disgraceful, exploitative, and ultimately *private* act of consensual sex. This seemed a sophisticated, level-headed, almost Continental reaction—but also a rather cynical one. The President was assumed, from the start, to be promiscuous. Starr was assumed to be political (and found to be a charmless fanatic). Politicians were assumed to be liars. The media were assumed to be craven and sensationalist.

Clinton had, as Broder maintained, surely disgraced the presidency, but that was only part of the story: Washington had disgraced itself. Twenty-five years of self-destructive, internecine stupidity had finally borne its fruit: The public was disgusted—in a vague, bored way—with almost everyone associated with public life.

In the end, I found two theories—one historical, the other spiritual—that helped explain the witless intensity of Washington's reaction to the Lewinsky scandal.

Years earlier, the Yale historian Stephen Skowronek had described Clinton, Richard Nixon, and Woodrow Wilson—as well as Andrew Johnson, John Tyler, Grover Cleveland, and Dwight Eisenhower—as Third Way presidents. The nomenclature was unintentionally ironic: Skowronek's "third-way" was different from Clinton's. Skowronek defined this sort of President as one who tended to appropriate his opponents' agenda and get it enacted after sanding off the rough edges (Wilson appropriated Theodore Roosevelt's Progressive program; Eisenhower was the first Republican to accept the assumptions of Franklin Roosevelt's New Deal). Such presidents are often mistrusted by their own party, and they are inevitably detested by the opposition, but they also tend to be quite successful: Each of Skowronek's Third Way presidents who chose to run for a second term won reelection (except Cleveland, who lost and then won again four years later). Success, however, was usually fleeting—"no 'third way' has ever outlasted the president who articulated it," Skowronek wrote years before Al Gore failed in his attempt to succeed Clinton.

Furthermore, the price of Third Way success was often a dangerously personal political atmosphere: "While other leaders might appear weak or even incompetent," Skowronek continued, "third-way presidents are often judged moral degenerates, congenitally incapable of rising above nihilism and manipulation." Even Woodrow Wilson—that perfect Presbyterian—was, Skowronek notes, subjected to an amazing assault by his predecessor, Theodore Roosevelt, who "mercilessly derided Wilson's adroit, unscrupulous cunning, his pandering to those who love ease . . . his readiness to about-face . . . his lack of all conviction and willingness to follow every gust of opinion."

Certainly, Clinton's political hermaphroditism had something to do with the excessive hatefulness that crippled his opponents. But beneath the politics, a more primal and even theological melodrama was at work: a temple riot, of sorts—a disturbance among the national priesthood, a scapegoat sacrifice. The Stanford University literature and religion scholar René Girard, whose book *Violence and the Sacred* explores the intense societal purposes of the scapegoat ritual in the ancient world, told me that Bill Clinton was a classic scapegoat—which is not to say that he was wrongly accused. Quite the opposite, in fact. In the ancient world, a scapegoat personified the pathologies of his society and his times. "In Greek mythology, the scapegoat is never wrongfully accused," Girard said. "But he is always magical. He has the capacity to relieve the burden of guilt from a society. This seems a basic human impulse. There is a need to consume scapegoats. It is the way tension is relieved and change takes place."

It seems likely, in retrospect, that Bill Clinton was a compendium of all that his accusers found most embarrassing, troubling, and loathsome about themselves, especially those who came of age, as he did, in the deep, narcotic prosperity that enveloped the nation after World War II. On the most superficial level, his excesses reflected the personal excesses—sexual and material—of his generation. Deeper down, his poll-obsessed administration often seemed the triumph of marketing over substance—which reflected nagging doubts about a nation dominated by a virtual economy of "concepts" and cyber-processes, rather than the substantive assembly lines that had provided the illusion of economic stability in the past. Finally, there was the free-range fudgery: Clinton had escaped military service in Vietnam. He had never sacrificed for his country. He had never been tested by adversity. He (and his doppelgänger, Gingrich, and his successor, George W. Bush) were relative dilettantes compared to the generation that preceded them—the generation of Bob Dole and Bob Michel and George H.W. Bush. A certain generational callowness needed to be exorcised.

But the Lewinsky affair was a scapegoat sacrifice that didn't work. There was no catharsis; the scapegoat escaped. And the tension remained in a society troubled by a vague, aimless emptiness—a tension attributable, perhaps, to the spiritual toll taken by the most spectacular prosperity in the history of the world.

In the end, Clinton's symbolic identification with the pathologies of his era may be destined to overwhelm the real accomplishments of his time in office.

CHAPTER

EIGHT

One of the odder stories of the Clinton years involves Ira Magaziner, who stayed on in the White House after the failure of his health insurance plan in 1994, hoping to rescue a bit of his reputation and do something useful before he left. "I was radioactive," he said later. "But the President offered me several projects. Most of them involved figuring out ways to harness new technology to promote economic growth. I decided to work on a set of rules to govern e-commerce on the Internet—which, in 1995, barely existed. Basically, everyone except for a few people on the economic team laughed and said, 'Well, if Magaziner wants to do that, great!' "

Magaziner decided to experiment. The methodology of the health care task force had been disastrous; he would do the opposite with e-commerce and see what happened. The process would be transparent, rather than secret. It would be bipartisan. He found conservative Republican partners, like Representative

Christopher Cox of California (who later told me, with some amazement, "On this issue, Ira and I think exactly alike."). He published his proposed e-commerce protocol on the Web, and asked for suggestions; the protocol went through fourteen public revisions before it was approved, and announced by Bill Clinton on July 1, 1997. Most striking, however, was the philosophy of Magaziner's approach. It was firmly Libertarian; not just anti-censorship—but also opposed to the imposition of a sales tax on cyber-purchases, as a way to encourage the growth of e-commerce. And so, Ira Magaziner became the unlikely father of the Internet's duty-free zone, a no-tax policy that was adopted internationally after Clinton proposed it (and which has become more controversial as e-commerce continues to grow, unencumbered by the burdens imposed upon traditional businesses).

It was also a policy that fit with the Administration's approach to other New Economy issues. This was an absolutely crucial—if deadly dull—area of policy-making: Gore country. The Clinton administration didn't create the information technology boom of the 1990s, of course; but it might have strangled the new economy through overregulation or by limiting competition (which was the course of action favored by many telecommunications industry lobbyists, who are among the most powerful in Washington). Instead, the White House—led by the Vice President, who really did have a passion for these issues—acted to encourage a free market in the emerging information technologies. Mobile phone services blossomed after the Federal Communications Commission auctioned the rights to a portion of the radio band dedicated to cellular use; the Internet boomed, in part, because the FCC ruled that connections could be made at the price of a local rather than a long-distance call; the Telecommunications Act of 1996 encouraged competition in both local and long-distance telephone markets. "Our new approach was to use the authority of the telecommunications law to rescind the compact between government and the status quo in the information sector," according to Reed Hundt, in a memoir of his time as Clinton's first chairman of the Federal Communications Commission. "Companies might fail, service might be interrupted, choice could confuse customers. But we would unleash the power of change."

The President wasn't particularly interested in these sorts of issues, at first. He remained cyber-impaired, far happier pressing the flesh than gazing at a computer screen, more likely to communicate by phone than by e-mail—unlike Al Gore and George W. Bush, both of whom had very active e-lives. But Clinton's ability to understand the changing economy, and to describe the impact of that change for average Americans, remained one reason why the public continued to trust him even after he had demonstrated his personal untrustworthiness.

In his second term, Clinton shifted his attention from domestic issues to postmodern, global questions—biomedical research, the AIDS epidemic, how Information Age technology could be put to use in the poorest villages. "He's as obsessed by those sorts of issues now," Donna Shalala told me, "as he was by health insurance and welfare reform when he came to the presidency."

Harold Varmus, Clinton's director of the National Institutes of Health, would never forget a White House meeting where the President grilled AIDS researchers for several hours, asking questions so detailed and sophisticated that most of the participants were shocked by his mastery of the issue. "He can tell you which cabinet ministers are good, and not so good, on AIDS in every African country," said Richard Holbrooke, who became equally obsessed with this issue when he served as Clinton's ambassador to the United Nations.

One global issue that Clinton did not address sufficiently, obviously, was terrorism. He never found a creative way to engage the increasingly secular government of Iran, which funded terrorists (like the Hezbollah in southern Lebanon), but also opposed the more radical Taliban government—and its guest, Osama bin Laden—in Afghanistan. He never figured out how to thwart Saddam Hussein's apparent efforts to create a stockpile of chemical and biological weapons. (It should be noted that the Clinton national security team tacitly accepted the first Bush administration's implicit policy in Iraq: Saddam in power was better than the instability that might occur if he was removed—Shiites, Sunnis, and Kurds splitting off into states of their own, which might, among other things, greatly strengthen Iran and pose a serious threat to the territorial integrity of Turkey.)

Terrorists slowly escalated their attacks on the United States throughout Clinton's second term. There was the June 25, 1996, attack on Khobar Towers, the American barracks in Saudi Arabia, in which 19 Americans were killed. There was the August 7, 1998, bombing of American embassies in Kenya and Tanzania, in which 263 people, mostly Africans, were killed. There was the October 12, 2000, assault on the *USS Cole*, in which 17 American sailors were killed.

"After Osama bin Laden's organization bombed the American embassies in Kenya and Tanzania, terrorism became my number-one priority," said Samuel Berger. "I believed that it was the single greatest threat. We worked on it every day—and we tried very hard to get bin Laden. We had excellent intelligence that there was an event, a meeting, that he would be attending with three or four hundred of his closest associates. We attacked with cruise missiles and we just missed him. By an hour, perhaps. I'm not sure. We never had a clear shot after that."

But there *were* other possible "shots" to be taken that were foiled by bureaucratic opposition. The most vexing concerned the use of cyber-warfare against the financial assets of terrorists and corrupt leaders who had looted their countries. Proposals were developed to electronically "lock up" bank accounts used by Slobodan Milosevic and, later, by bin Laden and others to finance terrorist activities. Treasury officials said that none of the accounts in question were very large, but that hardly seemed the point: It was estimated that the September 11, 2001, terror attacks cost no more than $500,000. "Those were the most frustrating conversations I've ever had in public service," said one of four Clinton administration officials who confirmed that the Treasuries Secretaries Robert Rubin and Lawrence Summers opposed cyber-warfare on the grounds that it might threaten the stability of the international financial system. This was not an unreasonable position, but the national security team argued back that bin Laden probably already had "sleepers" at work trying to wreak cyber-havoc on the American banking system. Samuel Berger was, apparently, the most forceful advocate of trying to choke off terrorist-related funds, but he could make no headway. "This was a neuralgic issue for Treasury," said one official.

After the terrorist attacks on the World Trade Center and the Pentagon, Berger remained diplomatic—though, one sensed, quietly fuming—as he refused to comment directly on the cyber-warfare discussions. But he did allow that "the risk equations have changed now. There are thresholds we can now break through—getting our allies to roll up networks they know about, opening up the banking system, greater intelligence sharing, greater cooperation with the Russians and others."

One major threshold immediately crossed by the Bush administration was the prevailing notion that terrorism was a law enforcement issue rather than a national security threat. "Before September 11, we had three terrorist attacks on America—the Khobar Towers bombing in 1996, the embassy bombings in 1998, the attack on the *USS Cole* in 2000—and in each case, the lead agency investigating the case was the FBI," said former senator Bob Kerrey, who served on the Senate Intelligence Committee through most of the 1990s. "To my mind, these were acts of war, not just law enforcement issues."

The relationship between Bill Clinton's White House and Louis J. Freeh's Federal Bureau of Investigation was notoriously rocky. For its part, the FBI was furious over the administration's unwillingness to push the Saudis to cooperate more fully in the Khobar Towers investigation. "You wonder why we didn't push harder," said Leslie H. Gelb, president of the Council on Foreign Relations. "You wonder why we didn't say to them, 'If you don't turn over the people we need to talk to, we're going to stop supplying you with military equipment.' "

But the Administration was pressured by other forces—American diplomats in Saudi Arabia, American oil companies—not to jeopardize the relationship with Saudi Arabia, and the Clinton security team was equally furious with the FBI. "Their standard line was that Osama bin Laden wasn't a serious domestic security threat," said one former Clinton official. "They said that bin Laden had about two hundred guys on the ground and they had drawn a bead on them. Actually, after the FBI broke up the millennium operation"—the attempt to bomb Los Angeles International Airport and perhaps other sites on New Year's Eve, 1999—"they had a fair amount of credibility. The other problem we had with the FBI was a real unwillingness to share information. They insisted upon a 'chain of custody.' In other words, if they shared information about, say, the activities of certain bin Laden cells, and the information was acted on by other government agencies, it could not be used later in court cases against the terrorists."

There was always *something*, it seemed, preventing the Clinton administration from taking effective action—the Pentagon, the Treasury, the friends of the Saudis, the FBI. These failures seem stark and indefensible in retrospect, but they occurred in a very different world. "The post–Cold War era ended on September 11, 2001," said Barry Posen, a defense-policy analyst at the Massachusetts Institute of Technology. "The days of an inattentive, inexpensive American global hegemony are over. We were lulled by the Gulf War, which represented the apotheosis of high-tech warfare. We believed we could get the job done from a great distance, with no casualties. People now talk about Bill Clinton's unwillingness to engage, to get down and dirty, and there is some validity to those arguments. But low-risk, long-distance assaults were all that the military, and many of our allies, would tolerate—and I didn't hear very many Republicans, with the possible exception of John McCain on Kosovo, screaming about the need for 'closework' then, either."

IN THE SPRING OF 2000, the President convened a White House conference on the New Economy and sat, deliriously happy, through a day of panels on topics ranging from the macroeconomics of the Information Age to the spirit of community in an increasingly "virtual" society. He chaired every panel, listening intently and asking smart questions—it was a bookend, in a way, to the daylong conference on the domestic economy that he had convened in Little Rock just after he was elected in 1992. Even at the end of the day, he seemed reluctant to stop talking. During the final panel about the social implications of the Internet—with the East Room of the White House nearly empty and panelists checking their watches—Clinton was still engaged, blissfully oblivious to the length of the program. He asked Robert Putnam of Harvard a telling question. Putnam's book *Bowling Alone* had started a debate about the declining importance of community activities, and Clinton was wondering about the social isolation of the Internet. He pointed out that eBay, the virtual auction house, had created a livelihood for thousands of new traders, some of whom had been on welfare before, "and that's a good thing," the President said, "but you have to wonder. These people are doing this work at home, alone. You have to wonder whether that has any long-term impact on the things we need to do together, as a society."

Afterward, the President stopped to chat with me about the

day. He was very excited, fizzy with ideas. He wanted to talk about a village he'd recently visited in India. There had been a computer and "they had this guy there who supervised it and printed out stuff from the Internet," he said, "and pregnant women were lined up, waiting to get the information they needed about prenatal care—can you imagine if we could get one of those into every village?"

The effervescent informality—his eyes wide open, eyebrows dancing; he had to be dragged away by aides—was classic Clinton. It was the same quality that made his titanic State of the Union addresses so compelling; it stood in brilliant contrast to the overprepared, cautious pomposity that deadened most political rhetoric (for example, the carefully read, and sometimes misread, pronouncements of the presidents who came directly before and directly after him). There was a fair amount of artifice to this public persona, of course: Almost everything Clinton said when a camera was pointed at him was pretested by Mark Penn. But even when he was fully prepped, Clinton could make it sound as if he was just chatting. At the heart of this skill was a very real enthusiasm—the man simply loved to talk—and an innate homing mechanism that enabled him to locate the killer anecdote, the memorable statistic that would make the most abstruse issues human and comprehensible. "There is a statistic the President used *years* ago that I just can't get out of my mind," recalled Zoe Baird, who became the president of the Markle Foundation, which has devoted much of its resources to Internet policy research. "When he first came to office and people were still really scared about the new economy, he would say, 'More people have been hired by companies owned by women in the past five years than have been laid off by the Fortune Five Hundred.' His ability to find and fix on things like that was a good part of his success in making the country comfortable with the global economy. He could always find the reassuring story that proved good things were about to happen."

Optimism is an extremely valuable, but often overlooked, political attribute. The Democrats became the party of positive thinking when Franklin D. Roosevelt assumed the presidency; the optimism was renewed by Harry Truman, made elegant by John F. Kennedy, and legislated by Lyndon Johnson. But Vietnam transformed them into a party of pessimists. Ronald Reagan, who'd been raised a New Deal Democrat, was the first post-Vietnam President to clearly understand this distinctly American strand of civic DNA: He proclaimed "Morning in America" as the theme of his 1984 campaign (Richard Gephardt responded in 1988, during his failed Democratic candidacy: "It's more like midnight."). Clinton saved the Democrats from their latter-day darkness with his optimism about America's multiracial culture, and about the possibilities of the global economy—and his ability to convince average Americans that these were opportunities, not threats.

Indeed, Clinton's public charm—his ability to talk, to empathize, to understand; his willingness to fall behind schedule, to infuriate his staff, merely because some stray citizen on a rope line had a problem or a story that needed to be heard—will doubtless stand as his most memorable quality. Senator Paul Wellstone of Minnesota, a liberal who believed that Clinton squandered a great opportunity for "social action," once told me a story about a friend of his, a school teacher named Dennis

Wadley, who was dying of cancer in 1994. "Dennis was a political junkie," Wellstone recalled, "and I arranged for him to meet the President just before he died. We met at the end of a day, at a local television station in Minneapolis. Clinton came right over to us and he immediately sized up the situation—Dennis didn't want to talk about his disease, he wanted to have a policy discussion. And the President stood there, for forty-five minutes, and gave Dennis the gift of taking him seriously, listening to him, responding intelligently. He never mentioned the illness. It was an incredibly gracious act, entirely natural. Effortless. This is the humanity that we didn't see reflected in the policy area."

Wellstone's wistfulness seemed universal among reasonable people. It came in different forms, from left, right, and center. But there was a pervasive sense of talent squandered, of a great opportunity wasted. Even many of Clinton's closest friends were disappointed by his performance as president; and yet, when these same people were asked what else Clinton might actually have accomplished, the answers were too specific to be quite right—universal health insurance, most often; reforming Social Security and Medicare; more money for education, according to Robert Reich. Worthy suggestions all, but insufficient to explain the larger sense of incompleteness that haunted the Clinton project.

Moral turpitude was part of the problem, of course. Even if Clinton had passed universal health insurance, tackled terrorism, solved the Middle East, and led a successful global effort against AIDS, the Lewinsky scandal—and the outrageous gush of pardons granted on his last night in office—would still cast an enduring shadow over his presidency. (At the same time, the Republican impeachment proceedings will stand as an inexplicable moment of self-destructive extremism, an act that will define the Gingrich "revolutionaries," just as the unnecessary impeachment of Andrew Johnson defined their "radical" Republican predecessors.)

The Lewinsky scandal had a powerful, if usually overlooked, impact on the substance of Clinton's last two years in office as well. When I asked the President what he might have accomplished absent the scandal, he said that he wasn't sure. When pressed, Clinton acknowledged that he might have been able to reform the Social Security and Medicare systems if the Republicans—and the media—hadn't been provided with an alternative form of diversion in 1998 and 1999. In fact, Clinton was poised, at the moment he delivered his "Save Social Security First" challenge in the 1998 State of the Union message, to do something few presidents ever had: to end his second term with a valedictory surge of significant accomplishments. He had tamed the Republican Congress. There were huge budget surpluses to play with. "Both parties were behind the curve on the big issues," said Bruce Reed, Clinton's domestic policy advisor. "Everyone had spent years thinking that real pain would be required to solve Social Security and Medicare. But we had the money to do it right then and there. We could have added a private-investment option on to Social Security benefits—the government could have matched voluntary contributions dollar-for-dollar for poor and middle-class taxpayers, as Gore proposed in the 2000 campaign. We could have brought Medicare up to date, and made it more efficient as well. But nobody on either side really wanted to do anything. There was Lewinsky. And many Democrats enjoyed using these 'entitlement' issues against Republicans. . . . Consequently, Bill Clinton may be the only leader in all of history to leave a budget surplus of such magnitude for his successor to figure out how to use."

In the end, Clinton's most significant policy failure may have been his inability to create a revised social safety net appropriate to the Information Age. This was a failure with significant generational resonance: the Baby Boomers were leaving an expensive demographic mess for their children. There was a need for new, sleeker systems—including universal health insurance—that would be customized, decentralized, more flexible than the creaking pension and health care programs of the Industrial Age, and more responsive to the velocity and turbulence of the new era. The failure to modernize Medicare was a particularly galling example of Clinton's inability to do the right thing after Lewinsky.

The outlines of a plausible Medicare reform—a system that would introduce competition, and also new benefits (like prescription drugs) to the notoriously inefficient and wildly expensive old-age health plan—had been prepared by Senators John Breaux of Louisiana and Bill Frist of Tennessee. This was, in a way, the latest iteration of the same old policy debate—the battle that had first been joined over day care in the 1980s—and the Breaux–Frist approach was well within the parameters of The Third Way. "That was the idea," said one of Clinton's closest advisors. "Breaux was our guy. We had a sense what was coming. Breaux–Frist needed a lot of work, but we could have done something with it."

But the Breaux–Frist proposal was unveiled in the spring of

1998, a moment when the President could not afford to offend liberal Democrats in the House of Representatives. Clinton wasn't entirely pleased with the plan, but he didn't have the energy or political wherewithal to massage it into shape and then create the bipartisan coalition to pass it, as he had done with welfare reform and NAFTA. So he simply opposed it, and lost all chance for Medicare reform. He never followed through on Social Security, either. Indeed, Clinton will be remembered more for his irresponsibility on these issues, for his willingness to exploit public fears about the loss of old-age entitlements— which he did egregiously, and inaccurately, during the government shutdown of 1995 and in the election of 1996—than for any effort he made to reform them.

There were also serious foreign policy consequences to the Lewinsky scandal. The cruise missile attack on a pharmaceutical factory in Sudan and a guerrilla encampment in Afghanistan— both sites allegedly connected with Osama bin Laden—took place on August 20, 1998, three days after the President's grand jury testimony in the Lewinsky case. There was another futile aerial bombardment of Iraq that commenced on December 16, just as Clinton was about to be impeached by the House of Representatives. The air campaign in Kosovo and Serbia began just after Clinton was exonerated by the United States Senate in February of 1999. All of these actions may have been limited, or prompted—certainly, they were influenced—by the President's personal difficulties. But it is unlikely, even if the Lewinsky affair had never happened, that Clinton would have mounted a campaign to lead the nation against the threat of overseas thuggery and sent American troops off to neutralize Slobodan Milosevic,

Saddam Hussein, or Osama bin Laden. The villains were egregious, but the threat was too distant, too uncertain. And the country was in no mood to be disturbed. Still, the overwhelming Monica distraction must have hindered Clinton's ability to do the careful preparation necessary for all three operations. And it showed.

There were other Lewinsky-related foreign policy consequences. In the spring of 1999, the President suddenly changed his position on the normalization of trade relations with China, a deal that his own trade representative, Charlene Barshefsky, had carefully negotiated—and which the Chinese Premier, Zhu Rongji, had traveled to the United States to ratify; the President did this, in part, to repay the liberal, protectionist Democrats in the House of Representatives who had just saved his presidency by making the impeachment proceedings a partisan vote, thereby stripping the process of any public credibility.

But Clinton was receiving some strange advice from within the West Wing as well: Al Gore and others urged him to delay the China deal, which they had long supported. Gore's caution here reflected what seemed almost an intellectual nervous breakdown as he approached his own moment of truth in the year 2000. He spent the last two years of his vice presidency skittering away from the moderate positions he had long advocated—a clumsy, and politically questionable, effort to make himself more acceptable to the party's left wing. But Gore was ecumenical in his cowardice: He also deemphasized the liberal, visionary position he had taken on the environment—which was, in a way, sadder still.

"Gore's last two years in the White House were every bit as

dreadful as Clinton's first two years," said an advisor close to both men. Gore's personal discomfort with Clinton had increased dramatically during the second term. There was the impact of the Lewinsky mess on his presidential campaign, of course (the fact that Gore had daughters Lewinsky's age made his outrage over the situation all the more vivid). But far more important was Gore's almost pathological need to prove that he could stand on his own, outside the shadow of the political master—and perhaps outside his father's shadow, as well; his pride and discomfort paralyzed his campaign, compounding his natural awkwardness. Clinton grew frustrated with Gore over time, too—frustrated that Gore seemed intent on pushing him aside, frustrated by the Vice President's mortal clunkiness as a campaigner. Indeed, Gore ran one of the most inept presidential campaigns of the television era. "I never understood," said a member of the Bush family, "why he didn't just turn to George in those debates and ask, 'Could you remind me, governor, just what is it about peace and prosperity you don't like?' "

(Normalization of trade relations with China passed in the spring of 2000, after a major lobbying effort by the President, who had reverted to his original position; but the humiliation of Zhu Rongji, which the Chinese saw as a major loss of face, and the carelessness inherent in the accidental bombing of the Chinese embassy in Belgrade during the Kosovo war, probably has strengthened those in Beijing who argue that the United States is not to be trusted.)

The President's need to shove Lewinsky into the background, to close his eight years with one last, improbable burst of historic achievements, may also have led him to press too hard for an

Israeli–Palestinian peace accord in the last summer of his presidency. He has since admitted that he misread the Palestinian leader Yasser Arafat's refusal to budge in the latter stages of the negotiations, that he figured Arafat would say yes after extracting every last possible concession from the Israelis—a truly disastrous miscalculation, both on Clinton's part and on the part of Israeli prime minister Ehud Barak, who believed that a deal with the Palestinians was the only way to save his own sagging political fortunes.

There are those who argue that the failure of Camp David was valuable in itself: It demonstrated the fundamental intransigence of the Palestinians and ended a dangerous period of Israeli delusion that began when Yitzhak Rabin shook Arafat's hand on the White House lawn. But that seems an unduly cynical view. Camp David also ended the happiest six years Israel had known as a nation, a time of prosperity and increasing contact with the rest of the world. The failure to make peace burst a precious, if precarious, status quo. An argument can be made that what Israel and the Palestinians needed most was the *appearance* of a peace process, rather than a forceful effort to close the deal. It is obvious, in retrospect, that Arafat wasn't prepared to accept any deal—a Palestinian "state" composed of Gaza and the detritus of the West Bank was hardly a state at all. Far more important, a peace agreement would have forced the Palestinians, and Arafat personally, to abandon the only true national identity ever shared by the ill-defined Arab peoples who lived on the territory designated a Jewish state in 1948. They would no longer be stateless victims (and it would have ratified the tragic reality that the Arabs who left in 1948 had no legal claim to their former homes; Clinton later said that the "right of return" was the real sticking point for the Palestinians). Furthermore, with peace concluded, Arafat would actually have had to *manage* a state—a far less exciting, and far more troublesome, occupation than dashing around the world harvesting money and sympathy from guilty Arabs and mortally squishy Europeans.

"Arafat feels more comfortable, and his strength is the greatest, when he can play the role of victim. He really knows how to do that well," Clinton said later, six months after he left office. It was an odd admission for a politician so emotionally astute: The Camp David agreement that Clinton sought would have required Yasser Arafat to stop being Yasser Arafat, an extremely unlikely capitulation.

The consequences of Clinton's Camp David effort were immediate and violent—a renewal of the *Intifada*; the fiercest, most violent run of terror bombings and Israeli military reprisals in a decade, which helped feed anti-Americanism in the Islamic world, and may have increased the romantic cachet of radicals like bin Laden; the fall of Barak's government and the election of Ariel Sharon as prime minister; a deeper, perhaps irreparable sense of pessimism on the part of both Israelis and Palestinians. And a lingering sense of guilt for Bill Clinton, guilt that he may have tried to exorcise on his last night in office, when he issued a presidential pardon to a gentleman named Marc Rich.

BILL CLINTON LEFT THE PRESIDENCY the same way he'd entered it: exhausted to the point of foolishness. Just as his failure to take a vacation after the election in 1992 had led to a series of slips and miscalculations (the "gays in the military" disaster, the decision to cave to the Democratic leaders on campaign finance reform), his need now to savor every last moment of his time in office led to an insomniacal frenzy—a whirling about the nation on Air Force One for a series of emotional farewells, the signing of a slew of executive orders (many of them environment-related, a departing slap at the corporatists who would succeed him), the negotiating of a plea bargain with the last Whitewater prosecutor Robert Ray and, finally, the granting of 177 presidential pardons and commutations of sentence on his last night in office.

There was a libidinous crudeness to all of this. It was a final self-indulgence, a total loss of control. Other presidents had granted last-minute pardons, had signed last-minute executive orders, had staged bathetic farewell tours—but the rapacious enormity of these conceits and absolutions seemed to recapitulate Clinton's most loathsome qualities. And the Marc Rich pardon, at once incomprehensible and instructive, was the worst of it all.

Rich was routinely described in the newspapers as a "fugitive financier." That seemed inadequate: This was no mere white-collar criminal. He evaded tens, perhaps hundreds, of millions of dollars in taxes. He traded oil, and perhaps arms, with America's enemies. He fled the country and renounced his citizenship. He was a grotesque, a caricature—sadly, inescapably, a Jewish caricature (particularly in his efforts to absolve his sins by slathering millions of dollars upon selected, often Israeli, charities)—and so was his foolish, tasteless former wife, Denise.

Denise Rich and her friend, Beth Dozoretz, seemed visitors

from the Middle Ages. They were courtiers, fluttering about the President, flattering him with praise and money. Rich contributed $450,000 to the Clinton Library, $100,000 to Hillary Clinton's Senate campaign, and $1 million to the Democratic Party; she also bought seven thousand dollars' worth of furniture for the Clinton home in Chappaqua, New York. Dozoretz worked tirelessly to raise funds for the Democratic Party and pledged to raise $1 million for the Clinton Library; she was checked through White House security a staggering ninety-six times during Clinton's last two years as President. Ehud Barak was a significant actor in the pardon as well: He called the President three times to plead for Rich (who had contributed mightily to Barak's campaign fund)—and Clinton later admitted that he gave undue weight to these conversations because he felt responsible for Barak's political fate. And then there was former White House Counsel Jack Quinn, who knew precisely how to advance a case in the Court of Clinton (he certainly knew the President's susceptibility to arguments about the indignities of prosecutorial fervor). But the emollient unctuousness of Denise Rich and Beth Dozoretz stood at the emotional heart of the matter.

"You know I'm not about money," the former President said to me about a month after he left office. And that was true: Clinton had been famously indifferent to personal affluence during his single-minded dash to the presidency. But this was a quality that became less important during his years in Washington, since the President lives the most regal of American lives (Clinton's financial modesty would be more severely tested in his post-presidency, since he now had to make enough money "to support a senator," as he admitted to me in the same conversation).

Even if Clinton's indifference to personal affluence is granted, he was not exactly a pillar of rectitude, either. Throughout his years in office, he was easily seduced by the promise of *political* money—that is, by contributions to his cause—and he was a total bimbo when it came to flattery. These had been Clinton weaknesses even before he'd achieved the presidency—his need to surround himself with sycophants; his susceptibility to scoundrels like Jim McDougal. The fierceness of the Republican assault had only intensified these tendencies. The need to raise money—for his reelection first, then for his legal defense fund, and finally for his library—breached the bounds of taste, if not legality; the need to be surrounded and reassured by adoring flunkies was equally intense. This was, in a way, the mirror image of his compassion: He not only had a compulsion to please others, but also to be fawned over himself. Indeed, that may have been the real quid pro quo of the Marc Rich pardon. It was a favor granted in return for indulgences.

There was an almost literary resonance to this final twist: The naked vehemence of his need to devour all the privileges of the presidency in his last days, the utter loss of political perspective, was Lewinsky redux. Both scandals seemed to confirm the worst suspicions about the sort of human being he was. In an odd way, Denise Rich and Beth Dozoretz and Monica Lewinsky were of a piece—desperate to please, desperate for attention, and easy to exploit. Clinton's eagerness to exploit them all (in different ways, of course) was imperious and manipulative; his willingness to be exploited in return, and the certain knowledge that the exploitation was bound to be exposed, was downright weird. In perhaps the most remarkable moment of his Starr testimony, Clinton said he assumed that Monica Lewinsky would not be able to keep the secret. So *why*, on earth, did he choose to proceed? Even the most sympathetic observer is left spluttering.

One imagines that other leaders—many of those remembered as great and caring, like Franklin Roosevelt and John F. Kennedy—were as selfish and needy and self-destructively strange as Bill Clinton proved himself to be. The will to power assumes a certain fanaticism, particularly in a democracy. But the public had been spared the squalor in the past.

From the start, this was a President too familiar for comfort. Too much was known about him, and Clinton didn't seem to mind that at all—indeed, he played to it. He admitted that his marriage was "not perfect." He said he "didn't inhale." He answered a question, on MTV, about his style of underwear. He could have said "none of your business" to all of these, but Clinton had a remarkably sophisticated understanding of the power of vicarious intimacy: He knew that the President now lived in the kitchens and family rooms of the nation as surely as he lived in the White House. He made the town meeting into a campaign vehicle as inevitable as the televised debate (indeed, he combined town meeting and presidential debate and made that a quadrennial ritual as well). He was interactive. You could ask him questions and he would surely answer.

But something was lost in the process, long before Lewinsky. And one wonders if the sense of disappointment engendered by Clinton's presidency might not have been just as powerful, if less focused, without the sex and the pardons. His immense talents invited higher standards and expectations than were needed at so placid a moment in history; he had the misfortune to serve at a time when greatness wasn't required. There was always the sneaking suspicion that Clinton was a bit bored, that he needed the thrill of a crisis—and that if the world didn't present him with a challenge, he'd create one for himself. One imagines that Clinton regrets that he was never really put to the test, and one wonders how he would have fared in a national emergency. No doubt, he would have relished the chance to do something crucial, like make "war" on terrorism and rouse the nation after the September 11, 2001, attacks. He certainly had the skills to lead. But Clinton may have lost a great deal of his moral authority well before Lewinsky by snuggling too close to us—by polling every last public whim, by trying so hard to please. It is entirely possible that the Clinton era will be remembered by historians primarily as the moment when the distance between the President and the public evaporated forever.

"I'm not sure that's such a bad thing," Clinton told me, at the end of one of our conversations. "We need to demystify the job. It is a *job*. . . . There's a lot to be said for showing up every day and pushing the rock up the hill. . . . If you're willing to win in inches as well as feet, a phenomenal amount of positive things can happen. . . . If you love your country and have something you want to do and you put together a good team, and you're willing to be relentless and exhaust yourself in the effort, the results will come."

This seemed a sad and defensive peroration.

The Natural

HE REMAINS THE MOST compelling politician of his generation, although that isn't saying very much. Think of the others: the first Baby Boom vice presidents, Dan Quayle and Al Gore (the latter, a serious man who wilted in the spotlight); the Speakers of the House, Newt Gingrich and Dennis Hastert (a former high school wrestling coach); the Senate Majority Leaders, Trent Lott (a former cheerleader) and Tom Daschle (a dogged, clever technician without much vision or pizzazz). And then there is Clinton's successor, George W. Bush—another former cheerleader and a man with a public presence that was uncertain, at best, before the terrorists struck, and only intermittently better afterward.

In England, Tony Blair (a former rock-music promoter) successfully pursued policies quite similar to Clinton's but without the scandals. He was elected Prime Minister twice, by overwhelming majorities, and yet he was not well loved by the public. His reelection campaign, in the spring after Clinton left office, was marked by widespread apathy—the lowest percentage of Britons voting since 1918—particularly among the young.

Few of these men had done much in life before politics. There was a collective immaturity, a weakness and smallness—of purpose, of spirit, of inspiration—that cannot be coincidental. The cheerleaders and other assorted dilettantes who took power in the late twentieth century seemed poseurs, children playing at adult games, particularly when compared to the generation that had gone before them. The transition from Bob Michel to Newt

Gingrich, from the modest veteran of World War II to the faux revolutionary who tried to turn democracy into war—a transition from competence to bombast—stands as a quiet reproach to a self-indulgent, self-important generation.

Why did Baby Boom politicians seem so inadequate? I suspect that there were at least three interrelated factors. The first and most obvious is that they were, quite simply, untested—at least, until September 2001. They lacked the depth and breadth and wisdom that severe hardships bring. Few of them had experienced the loss of life and desperate uncertainty, the impossible decisions, and selfless sacrifice that is integral to the fabric of life in difficult times (this is one of the reasons why Vietnam veterans like John McCain seemed so much more compelling than other politicians of their generation). Once, early in the Clinton administration, I asked Lloyd Bentsen—an Army pilot who had flown the maximum missions allowed and been shot down in World War II—about the difference between John F. Kennedy's White House and Clinton's, which was to say, the difference between Bentsen's generation and mine. With great reluctance, the Treasury Secretary shook his head sadly and said, "I guess we didn't feel we had as much to prove."

Affluence—the deeply padded, peaceful security of the late twentieth century—also contributed to the prevailing callowness. Greatness in politics is rarely self-created; it is a consequence of trouble in the world. A leader without a crisis is usually consigned to the periphery of history (Theodore Roosevelt, who reinvented the American presidency by force of his personality in peaceful times, is an exception to this rule; there

aren't many others). The public doesn't ask much from politicians at such moments—people mostly want to be left alone.
Such apathy may or may not have longterm consequences for a
society; Machiavelli, among others, worried about it. He wondered how governments could keep their rigor—their moral authority—in times of peace. In the early sixteenth century, he
wrote that *ozio*—indolence—was the greatest enemy of a republic.

And so, one of the more subtle challenges facing George W.
Bush was the need to create a new, sustained level of public vigi-
lance—and just plain citizenship—to meet the challenge of a
conflict that would, by its very definition, be vague and intermittent, a conflict that might well become a permanent feature
of the civic landscape. He would have to do nothing less than
rescue the very notion of *leadership* from the grip of the professional image makers, a daunting task for a man whose political
successes had been so dependent on the skills of others.

Marketing has been the most insidious force in the shrinking
of public life. The ubiquitous pollsters and advertising consultants who dominated late-twentieth-century politics were thuddingly pragmatic. They asked people what they wanted. The
answers were always predictable: better schools, better health
care, safer streets—and lower taxes. And so, the politicians
themselves became thuddingly pragmatic. They became followers, not leaders—the most slavish, craven sort of followers, trail-
ing desperately after the whims and wisps of public opinion as
discerned by their pollsters and media consultants. Their messages tended to congeal in the safest, most conservative precincts

of the political middle, without any of the spontaneous brilliance and stray eccentricities and unplanned moments of courage that sparkle when a true leader is at work.

By the presidential campaign in 2000, the game had become so finely honed that the competing political "products" seemed generic. George W. Bush and Al Gore both offered prescription drug plans for older people and education plans for younger people; the plans were indistinguishable to all but the most discerning experts. Mushy oxymorons abounded. George Bush promised "compassionate conservatism." Al Gore promised "pragmatic idealism." Neither promised anything remotely resembling leadership—neither tried to rouse or inspire the public; and the public responded with an appropriately indifferent citizenship. "People just aren't interested in inspiration," the Republican pollster Frank Luntz told me in the midst of the campaign. "There is no desire for a call to action. People are focused on their own lives, their own neighborhoods. They lived through great political crusades—in 1992 and 1994—and both proved to be very disappointing. After Clinton and Gingrich, there is charisma fatigue."

It may stand as one of the great ironies of history that the personality trait least emphasized during the 2000 campaign—the ability to inspire, to lead—became the essential challenge for the new, well-intentioned, but profoundly unprepared President. True leadership can be a frightening thing for a politician. It is not something that can be tested in advance. It happens in the moment—in the arena, as Theodore Roosevelt said—and it is often inconvenient. An outrage, like the attacks on the World Trade Center and the Pentagon, will rouse and unite a people, but only real leadership can sustain a national sense of purpose. Usually, the tough decisions that a scrupulous leader must impose on the public don't "poll" all that well (think about the early public attitudes toward the Gulf War, the Bosnia intervention, the Mexican bailout). True leadership requires a leap of faith. It asks people to grow, to think about things they haven't thought about before, and sometimes, even, to sacrifice for the common good. This is a mysterious, atavistic force—an emotional bond—that can be easily perverted by demagogues. But there is a powerful, subterranean yearning, one suspects, for a President who knows more than the public does, who has a sense of what comes next, who will tell inconvenient truths, who will convince people—even the complacent and cynical inhabitants of the most successful country in history—that there is a real spiritual satisfaction to being part of something larger than themselves. Prior to the September attacks, the nation had lost the habit of all but the most convenient forms of patriotism. The public outpouring of support after the attacks was extraordinary, but it was also reflexive and perhaps short-lived; shepherding the country toward a more sustained, sober patriotism will be a daunting task for the new President.

DEEP IN THE AFFLUENCE AND lethargy of the late twentieth century, I once stumbled across an astonishing fact during a conversation with Mark Penn. I was asking about the damage to Clinton's reputation that had resulted from the campaign finance "scandal," the selling of the Lincoln bedroom and the White House parties for big donors. "Practically none,"

Penn scoffed. "Those stories had a penetration rate of only eight percent. If you want a point of comparison, the attempt to land a spacecraft on Mars had a penetration rate of ninety-three percent."

This may seem frivolous compared to the awful events—and the new, less secure reality—that overtook the nation at the beginning of the twenty-first century, but there was a lesson here about the inchoate public need for a sense of unity and purpose, even in times of peace. As John F. Kennedy found in the 1960s, there is a certain amount of civic passion inherent in a national effort to explore the universe—or a national effort to do anything else that is deemed worthy. There is a tacit public acknowledgment that government is the agency best equipped to do big things (it was no accident that on the day of the terror attacks, George W. Bush and members of his administration suddenly began referring to "your" federal government, a formulation that would have horrified many conservatives in the late twentieth century). Finally, there is great social value to the national sense of identity and purpose that comes from having a common goal. People are inspired. Children learn the possibility of heroism. Families talk about these things. The public square is filled with something other than rant.

Bill Clinton clearly understood this, in ways great and small, as no other politician of his generation did. No doubt, he will spend the rest of his days wondering how he might have handled the international crisis that was visited upon his successor. His frequent use of John Kennedy's hortatory salutation, "My fellow Americans," signaled that he aspired to something more ambitious than just sitting in the big chair. In 1992, his best moments as a candidate—and his biggest applause lines—came not when he made promises or criticized the opposition, but when he proposed a higher calling for young people, a new form of national service. There was enormous visceral power to this notion: It raised the possibility that the next generations could have the very experience that their Baby Boomer parents had missed—the opportunity to give intensive, all-consuming service to their country, to test their altruism against reality in the poorest of neighborhoods; it offered, in a way, the moral equivalent of war. And there was a significant political dividend in it for Clinton. National service was an issue that helped distinguish an obscure governor of Arkansas from his opponents. Audiences loved it, especially young audiences (although, in the late twentieth century, young audiences had become a rather rare political phenomenon—politics was rapidly becoming the exclusive province of the old). It reminded people of Kennedy and made Clinton seem larger—large enough, ultimately, to unseat the incumbent President of the United States.

A curious thing happened when the program was implemented, though. AmeriCorps turned out to be a worthy venture, one that Clinton's successor, George W. Bush, wisely chose to continue. But it lacked the drama and importance—the centrality—of Clinton's original campaign proposal (in part because the legislation was watered down, the opportunities for service made more peripheral, after pressure from the public employees unions). The President himself seemed to lose track of it after he came to office. There was just too much else going on. There was an ambitious deficit reduction plan to push through a recalcitrant Congress. There was health care. There was Bosnia.

There was welfare reform. There were the Republicans; there were the media. There wasn't time to think about how best to educate, much less inspire, the public—and how best to act—on other complicated issues like global warming or the international AIDS epidemic or the growing terrorist threat, either. Instead, a flawed and unenforceable treaty on global warming was negotiated at Kyoto (and then discarded by Clinton's successor). And the Congress grudgingly passed money to send medical supplies to Africa. And missiles were lobbed, from great distances, in the general direction of terrorists. But these were gestures, not actions. And the sense that the Clinton presidency was more about gestures—about "spin"—than about true leadership is at the heart of the disappointment his supporters feel. This is understandable. By his intelligence and remarkable political skills, by his detailed knowledge of almost every government activity, by his very presence, Clinton appeared to be promising greater things than he could ever deliver—in fact, nothing less than a political renaissance, a return to the days when public affairs seemed central to the life of the republic, when government was seen as a moral force, when politicians were assumed to be wise rather than corrupt. If Ronald Reagan had challenged the pessimism of the post-Vietnam era, liberals hoped that Bill Clinton would challenge the cynicism.

In the end, cynicism won—with a major assist from Clinton himself. But amid the dashed hopes and the scandals and the bitterness, a great deal of real work was done. Bill Clinton conducted a serious, substantive presidency; his domestic policy achievements were not inconsiderable and were accomplished against great odds. He had rescued the Democratic Party from irrelevance and pursued a new philosophy of governance that made public-sector activism plausible once more, even in a time of national apathy and skepticism. Moreover, he performed the most important service that a leader can provide: He saw the world clearly and reacted prudently to the challenges he faced; he explained a complicated economic transformation to the American people and brought them to the edge of a new era.

But he had hoped to do so much more—and now, in a final twist of fate, his public service may be defined by the smug, shallow serenity of his time: He may be remembered as the President who served before history resumed its contentious dance, before life got serious again.

Acknowledgments

Let us now praise famous editors. Peter Gethers and Bill Thomas of Doubleday, of course. David Remnick, Dorothy Wickenden, Jeff Frank, and John Bennet of *The New Yorker* (Wickenden, the toughest editor on the planet, was there at *Newsweek,* too—along with Mark Whitaker and Jon Meacham); and Paul Solman, who was the first to tell me that I might have a future in journalism, way back when at *The Real Paper.* But I'd particularly like to acknowledge the two editors who really taught me how to cover politics—Ed Kosner, who hired me to write a political column at *New York* magazine, and the late Maynard Parker of *Newsweek.* Both men encouraged me to take risks, have fun, and rant at will; both indulged my journeys to the arcane shores of social policy and my occasional need to write about obscure programs that actually worked (like Chilean social security reform and St. Elizabeth's School on the South Side of Chicago). Kosner had—and continues to have, as the editor of the *New York Daily News*—the clearest sense of how to attack a story of any editor I've ever known. Parker's willingness to remake an entire magazine at the last minute, and his insistence that I sometimes toss perfectly acceptable columns in order to get closer to late-breaking events, was similarly instructive. Both men had a sly sense of editorial naughtiness, which sometimes got us into trouble. I will always be grateful to Maynard for keeping the secret of *Primary Colors,* and will always regret that I did not understand the pain it would cause us both when I allowed it to go on so long.

Acknowledgments

I am not going to thank my sources within the Clinton and the two Bush administrations. You know who you are. I would, however, like to thank both President and Senator Clinton for their cooperation—and for a most exhilarating ride. Kathy Robbins, agent and pal, has always been there, with constructive criticism and encouragement. I'd also like to thank my sons, Chris and Terry Klein, for all of their advice and comfort over the years. And, of course, Victoria—talk about naughty and clever and fun: The Natural in my life.

Index

Index

Index

Index

Index

Index

Index

Index

Index

Index

About the Author

© PETER COVE

Joe Klein is the author of the novels *Primary Colors* and *The Running Mate,* and also two nonfiction books—*Woody Guthrie: A Life* and *Payback: Five Marines After Vietnam.*